The Unexpected Gift

By Michelle Schreder

VMI Publishers
Sisters, Oregon

Published by
VMI Publishers
Sisters, Oregon
www.vmipublishers.com
ISBN 0-9747190-21

Printed in the United States of America

CONTENTS

For Daniel and Jonathan -
I love you and God loves you more.
You are a tremendous gift!

ACKNOWLEDGMENTS

Who to acknowledge first? There have been so many people who have helped in the making of this book, either through prayer, encouragement or both. I am deeply indebted to them.

I suppose it would be most fitting to thank first my family; my boys, Daniel and Jonathan, who "consented" to let me "tell about them"; and to my husband, Jim, who never said I couldn't do this. Thanks for giving me the time and the space to "hole up" in the den and hog the computer. Thanks, too, to the grandparents who accept the kids for who they are and to my sister-in-law, Cate, with whom I trade email stories from the trenches, and on being "Mothers of the Year."

This book wouldn't be what it is without the moms who let me ask them a whole bunch of personal questions about their kids and their lives. Thanks to Kay, Gayle, Claudia, Barb, Ruth, Cindi, Julie and all the other moms (and dads) who are a part of the MoKSN group—your prayers and encouragement are invaluable. Thank you for being brave and vulnerable and real. Special thanks, to my friend, Connie, who not only listens to me with kindred heart, but who never stopped believing that this book could be written. Where would I be without you?

Many thanks to all the women of New Community, who prayed, sent notes, and listened to me when I needed to spill tears and words. A special thank you goes to Robin, Laurie, Karene, Laurene, Phyllis, Kathy, Nancy M., Nancy W., Janny, Margie B., Marie, Paula, Susan B, and Taimi. There are so many other women to thank; if I listed everyone this acknowledgement section would be a companion booklet. If you are not listed, be assured that you are not forgotten. The ladies of New Community truly embody what it means to be Christ's hands and feet—I love you all.

A million thanks to my "sister friends" Lisa and Barbara who've known me before I had a car, or a husband, and who have watched me attempt this thing called "motherhood." You let me be transparent—thanks for not telling me to stop whining when you could have, for not telling me to stop crying when I couldn't have, and for never saying anything when I wore those same black pants for two years straight. You've encouraged me by loving me and my kids unconditionally, and humored me by saying you could hardly wait to read this book. I can't tell you how much you mean to me—you guys rock!

Thanks, too, to my friends; Cheryl, who got the lowdown every morning on our way down to the lake—thanks for the therapy! Thank you to Shelia who knows what it feels like to have your world turned upside down, and who knows what joy is—thanks for all those nights spent getting coffee! Thanks to my buddy, Lori, who loves to read and be alone as much as I do—where would be with email? Thanks, too, to everyone in the FEFC orchestra; you encouraged me through prayer and email and hugs, and by listening to me "kvetch" a lot. Even though a lot of you didn't know this book was being written you'll never know how much you helped me!

To Jonathan and Daniel's teachers and therapists, there are not adequate words to express what you've given our family. Miss Patty and Trisha, did I ever tell you how jealous I was when you could make my boy do things I couldn't? You loved him and worked with him and never gave up. God gave you to us. And to the entire teaching and administrative staff at Fairmont Elementary School and Yorba Linda Middle, you are awesome. Though the school is huge, you always made room for those with special needs, and for us. We prayed every year to get just the right teachers, and we did. We prayed for the right speech therapists, psychologists and resource program specialists and we got those, too! Thank you, thank you, thank you—it's been one less battle for us to fight in our war.

And to Wendy Peterson, thanks for all your hard work in editing my first rough draft and subsequent revisions. This book isn't the same because of you—and that's good. You asked the right questions, encouraged me to explore new avenues, and pushed me to expand on ideas. Thanks for sharing late nights, weak tea, and laughs—maybe that funny disability book isn't such a bad idea after all!

Of course, the most thanks goes to my God, whose idea this was in the first place. Thank you for giving me the privilege of parenting the two most unique and beautiful boys on the planet. Thank you for all the special gifts you give each one of us. "Great things He hath taught us, great things He hath done, And great our rejoicing thro' Jesus the Son; But purer, and higher, and greater will be Our wonder, our transport, when Jesus we see." (To God Be the Glory-Fanny   Crosby)

Michelle Schreder Originally, May 6, 2001 Updated May 7, 2004

INTRODUCTION

Why This Book?

After visiting the local Christian bookstore for the third time, I almost walked out empty-handed again. This time, though, I felt compelled to ask the clerk if she could search for the subject I was looking for on the book list. "Do you have any books on raising children with disabilities, written from a Christian perspective? I don't need a how-to book. I need one that addresses my spiritual concerns and questions."

She paused and looked at me for a moment and tears came to her eyes. "There isn't one like that that I know of," she said softly. "My son is also disabled. He is an adult now. I wish that there was the kind of book you talked about."

We chatted for several minutes about our children, about our struggles as parents, and about our faith. Those moments were sweet. Still, I wished I had something written in hand. Guess I would just have to wait until somebody wrote something. But as I pushed on the door handle to exit, the most distinct voice sounded in my head: "You write it."

Over time, meetings with other moms of kids with special needs confirmed this call to put together a manuscript. In listening to each other's stories and concerns, we discovered that we have many of the same sorrows, frustrations, and questions of God that we don't always feel comfortable talking about with our other brothers and sisters in Christ. We fear not being "appropriate" or not "being a godly example." Within the safe walls of our conversations, however, we could ask and say things we "shouldn't." I suspect that many Christian parents of disabled children feel the same way.

These discussions with other parents helped shape the tone of this book. While some speak directly through their quoted stories, many of their voices are woven more indirectly into the fabric of the book through comments and conversations I have overheard or taken part in. While each parent I meet often has a different perspective or philosophy, we all find common ground in our experiences. I can meet a stranger and within five minutes find myself saying, "You too? Doesn't that drive you crazy? What do you do when . . . ?" This person may not know Christ yet, but through our children we are part of a special club, one we never volunteered to be in. We often find ourselves saying, "I don't think anybody knows what this is like. Don't you wish people knew? Maybe they would understand our children better."

Still, the task of writing about parenting the child with special needs, and its impact on my faith in Christ, felt beyond my scope. At times I wondered why in the world I ever started such a project. It's like having the world's longest term paper hanging over your head—except you don't ever get a grade or pass a class. I worried that I would offend people. I worried that I would spend all this time writing and that it would never get to print. Then I worried it would get to print and people would read all about our struggles and questions and draw the wrong conclusions.

But after talking with several godly counselor-friends, we came to the conclusion that this is actually God's project. If He wanted a book in print, He would send help. And He did so through the prayers and encouragement of many people and through leading me to passages in His Word I wouldn't have thought of on my own. So, if this book is in your hands, praise God the Almighty, because He did it!

The whole point of this book is to encourage parents of children with special needs to continue in their daily walk with God and hang tough when things feel hopeless. If ever anyone can understand looking through a mirror darkly, it's the parent of a child with disabilities. The incentive to work hard at parenting to "ensure productive members of society" is often diminished by the questions we have about our children's futures. Will they ever be able to live alone? Will they ever get a job? For some parents, the answer is already known, and it is not comforting. Could God have meant this to happen to us and to our child?

I am not an expert on disability; I am just a parent. I am also not a theologian, just a disciple of Christ. In fact, I am not even a writer but just a person who writes. I want other parents of children with special needs to know that they are not alone. Others just like you wonder, "How am I going to make it for an entire lifetime of parenting my special child? Does God have any idea how hard this is?" There are days when it seems that everything is too hard and nothing makes sense and we scream out, "Why?" Maybe we get an answer to our question; maybe we don't. I believe we should keep asking the questions but never stop exploring God's Word. He can speak to us through our pain and our questions. And He really wants to, because He really wants an honest, close relationship with us.

I also hope this book will help those who don't quite know what to do with their friends and family members who have a child with special needs to understand what we are about. I hope that others within the body of Christ, as well as those on the outside, will know that families with disability are not mistakes. We are ordained to be here, as hard as that is for anyone, including us, to imagine at times. We aren't just here to be ministered to; we are here to minister to you. Let us show you how. I guarantee you; it's not what you expected.

February 18, 2002

The Unexpected Gift

CHAPTER 1

Not What We Expected

My soul, wait thou only upon God; for my expectation is from him.

(Ps. 62:5 KJV)

The woman was well-dressed and very attractive; someone who would easily draw the admiring looks of others. She pushed a stroller through an upscale shopping mall that was located near a children's hospital. Anyone who has ever pushed a stroller will recall that it somehow becomes "open season" for total strangers to come up and start a conversation with you—"How old is the baby? Is it a boy or a girl? Shouldn't he be wearing a sweater?"

No one, though, was approaching this woman. People actually seemed to be cutting a wide swath around her as she maneuvered through the aisles. The universal law of "It's a Baby; It's Public Property" wasn't being followed. What was going on?

I peered inside the stroller and saw a boy who was about two years old, maybe older, who had a pronounced case of hydrocephaly. A shunt protruded from his enlarged head, which he had difficulty holding up. He was slumped over, gazing at nothing in particular.

I wondered if this mother and child were killing time at the mall before a neurologist's appointment. Was the little boy facing more surgery? The placid look on the mother's face masked whatever tension she may have been feeling. I wanted to catch her eye and give her a smile, but her attention remained fixed on the clothes rack in front of her.

About a year earlier, I had been the mother most strangers avoided. My younger son had a large scar running across his head from ear to ear after neurological surgery. For some reason, the doctor used what looked like black fishing line to sew up the wound, and coupled with the bruising and trauma that resulted from the surgery, my infant son's head looked kind of scary. Maybe if he would have allowed us to keep a bandage or hat on his head, instead of constantly pulling it off, the scarring could have remained hidden. But he refused to keep anything on his head, and his appearance definitely discouraged typical baby-banter from strangers. Inside, I wished people would have at least acknowledged my presence or felt free to ask me why it looked like my baby had a large zipper running across his head. But it was less awkward, I guess, for others to whisper and stare from a distance.

People were looking at this woman's young child and then quickly turning away, some sneaking a second look through downcast eyes. No one said hello to her or her son—in fact, no one even looked at her. And she had perfected the "I see you staring at my child but I'm pretending not to notice" nonchalance. The boy was well-dressed and in a fancy, expensive stroller. It seemed to me that she took great pains to make sure they both looked their best—this mom obviously cared about her son. He was her child and he was precious to her—just as my baby was beautiful and precious to me, despite his imposing scar.

Was anybody else aware of that, though? To the other mall-goers, the boy with the shunt was a curiosity at best, something to shield themselves from at worst.

He definitely wasn't what they had expected.

When the Unexpected Hits

Let's be honest, having a child or children with special needs isn't exactly what we expected for our lives either. Most of us probably imagined that we'd fall in love, get married, raise happy and successful children, see them get married and have children of their own, and then comfortably retire to a healthy and content old age. At least, that's the usual dream, right?

A child with special needs? That happens to other people. That's not what we want for our lives or for the children we dream of. It's something we may have feared or fought, like Barb, the mom of a child with multiple special needs:

> *About fifteen years ago, before we had kids, I worked with disabled adults while going to school. At that time, I swore the only thing in life I couldn't handle was having a child with a disability. I can remember telling the Lord, I'd rather go on the mission field than have to deal with a disability like the ones of the families I was dealing with. It began to weigh on my heart so much that I can remember sharing it with a few close friends. And I began arguing with God as to why I would make a much better missionary.*

Have you ever had a talk with the Lord like that? I have. About ten years ago, I was watching a PBS documentary on autism. I was horrified at a disability where the child seemed to slip away emotionally, intellectually, and verbally. What struck me most was the look on the parents' faces as they were being interviewed—a look of utter exhaustion and hopelessness, while their child was screaming and banging his body on the wall behind them. I whispered, "Oh, Lord, any disability but that one; I could handle any disability You might give us but autism"—as if any disability would be easy to handle!

I glanced over at my then one-year-old son, wondering if it was possible that he could slip into nothingness. I did not imagine that more than a decade later, he would indeed be diagnosed with autism. Nor did I imagine that his unborn brother, a child we hadn't even imagined yet, would also be diagnosed with the same disability.

I still wonder to this day what exactly God thought when I begged, "No, not us!"

What's your story? Did it ever enter your mind that you might have a child with disabilities? Did you argue with God as well? Since your child was born, have you struggled with disappointment . . . in yourself, in your child, even in God? Rest assured, you're not alone, not strange, and certainly not faithless. This life God has given us—and I do believe He chose it for us—is a hard one, often with little relief in sight. It's not what we expected, dreamed of, hoped for. Yet it's the one that God has given us. And He, more than we can imagine, knows the confusion, weariness, and sadness we sometimes feel. So He works with us, strengthening us, teaching us, loving us through it all.

That is, if we let Him.

Struggling with Unfulfilled Expectations

Most parents, myself included, eagerly anticipated the birth of our children. We pictured sunny days filled with laughter and love, and playtimes filled with fun and learning. Those of us who are athletic probably imagined teaching our kids how to hit a ball or how to somersault off of a diving board. We might have envisioned sharing our love of books or music or animals or the great outdoors. Or maybe we hoped our children would excel where we didn't, dreaming that they would do better in school than we did—maybe even becoming the class valedictorian!

In our minds, we would be able to call ourselves successful parents when our children finally accomplished all that we had dreamed for them. Our lives would be validated by what our children would become.

Where do these expectations leave us, though, when our child is born with disabilities? What sort of future do we have to look forward to? What kind of a present do we have to deal with?

Our dreams can seem like so many shards of broken glass when other parents are rejoicing over their children's great report cards and our son or daughter of the same age has just become toilet trained or has just learned how to tie a shoe. Our hearts easily get cut on the broken remnants even when other parents are complaining about their kids—their children are too noisy, too busy; while our children cannot talk or move.

We're good people, we may think, why didn't we get the healthy, happy children? When I discovered that the child I thought I "deserved" was different from the one I received, I felt as though something had been taken from me. "This isn't fair!" I cried out to God. "This happens to other people—people better equipped to handle this than I am."

In reality, though, there's no such thing as "people better equipped." Some of us may have better financial resources, but we all struggle with the physical and emotional drain of caring for a child with disabilities.

It may be meant as an encouragement, but the saying "God only gives special children to special people" rings hollow in the face of real-life experience. The demands of caring for a child with special needs, coupled with other family stresses such as divorce, financial strain, and substance abuse, are often enough to send even the "strongest" parent over the brink. This reality is often a hidden secret of families who struggle to care for a member with a disability.

The truth of the matter is that we are not "special people"; we are ordinary, fallible saints-in-training like all of God's children. And we need His help in coping with His changes in our plans.

Our Plans vs. God's Plans

Ironically, the One we need most is often the One we resist most. We're hurt…confused…angry. If God is all-powerful and all-loving, we reason, why would He do this to our children, to us? Why didn't He prevent the disabilities from forming? Where is His mercy? His kindness? Unless we drank, took drugs, or exposed our developing baby to something else harmful, we can't understand why this has happened.

And how do we talk about these thoughts with others? We need to wrestle through these hard questions, yet we fear that by doing so we will damage our Christian witness. If we aren't confident and joyful about our future, that may reflect badly on our faith. Sometimes it feels like being a Christian complicates our task of parenting a child with disabilities rather than helping us with it.

Yet, God understands our anger. He knows our pain. And He wasn't looking the other way when our child became disabled. He is all-powerful and all-loving—and He is also inscrutable. He has allowed us the privilege and the pain of parenting a special child for reasons that we may never understand on this earth. One of the most helpful things we can learn to do, then, is to learn to stop asking why. We need to learn to accept what we have been given and learn to move forward from there.

But to where? Where do we go from here? I think we need to go to at least two places.

First, we need to get to the place where we realize that God's blessings are not our rights. Health—ours and our child's—success, marriage, even life itself are gifts from God's hand. They are not things we have earned or deserved. They come by His grace and through His wisdom. And in His grace and wisdom, He has given us children who are precious in His sight, children who are more vulnerable and needy than other children.

That brings me to the second place we need to reach: a place of trusting God. He knows this is not easy for us. From our perspective, our future doesn't look very promising, so it is hard to believe that God knows what is best for us. After all, we know ourselves pretty well, don't we? We know what we can handle and what we can't (or we think we do). We know we don't always have a lot of patience or money or help from our spouse. We don't have training in neurology. We don't have nerves of steel. How will we maintain the energy to keep up with the appointments—the paperwork—our child's sleeplessness? Where will we get the strength to wrestle with the wheelchair and lift our child into it? How can we possibly teach our children to make it in the world, when that world doesn't welcome them as they are? In short, how do we learn to trust the One who we felt has let us down?

I don't have any easy answers. But I do know that the testimony of Scripture bears out the truth that God is worthy of our trust. His character is flawless and, from the witness of Christ's life, death, and resurrection, He cares deeply and is intimately involved with us. Even to an unfaithful nation that would soon reel under His righteous judgment, He gave this timelessly encouraging promise:

> *"I know the plans I have for you," declares the LORD,*
> *"plans to prosper you and not to harm you, plans to*
> *give you hope and a future." (Jer. 29:11)*

By learning to relinquish our resentment and reach out in trust, we will be able to see that our children are not unexpected disappointments but truly good gifts from our Father's gracious hand.

God's Unexpected Gift

Psalm 127:3—5 clarifies what blessings children are:

Behold, children are a gift of the LORD,
The fruit of the womb is a reward.
Like arrows in the hand of a warrior,
So are the children of one's youth.
How blessed is the man whose quiver
is full of them;
They will not be ashamed
When they speak with their enemies in the gate. (NASB)

Did you notice something? There are no qualifiers in this passage. All children are a gift from God. Not just the cute ones, the smart ones, and the healthy ones—but also the not-so-attractive ones, the delayed ones, and the ill ones. The child in the wheelchair is a blessing, and so is the one with the shunt coming out of her head. The child who doesn't speak is a blessing, and so is the one who doesn't hear. The child who obsesses and the child who stays up all night, the child who seizes and the child who drools—all children are a present to us from the One who delights in giving gifts.

Not only are they a gift, they are a reward. (Sometimes it's hard to remember that when they're screaming in the middle of the night!) Whether we are given this reward through birth or adoption, we are blessed to have children. Ask any couple who has known the grief of infertility and sought a child through adoption, and they will tell you that the pain and cost pales when compared with the joy of finally holding a new life in their arms.

How often, though, all parents take their children for granted or view them as a burden or a curse. This can be an especially hard struggle for parents with children with disabilities. We may not have received the child we had envisioned, but now we must reconcile our thwarted desires with what our reality is. We must temper our disappointment over the loss of the child we asked for with the knowledge that we have still been given someone who is indeed precious. We have received not just a disability but the gift of life itself.

What we need to learn as parents of children with special needs is how to enjoy this gift of life. It may seem impossible when we are waiting in yet another doctor's waiting room, cleaning out a feeding tube, or changing another diaper on a child well past toddler stage. But the Giver of gifts makes no mistakes. He is life; and when we appreciate the life He has entrusted to us, we come to know Him and live in His life so much better.

In the following pages, I hope that you, as a parent of a child with special needs, will find encouragement and strength for your parenting journey. Having a child with special needs can have a significant emotional and spiritual impact on your family—one that isn't always easy to talk about. With the help of stories from other families with children who have disabilities, may you see that you are not alone in your struggles. And I also hope that, with Scripture's encouragement, you will gain a greater understanding of the depth of God's love for you and your child. We have a great Advocate, not only for ourselves but for our children, in our Lord Jesus Christ.

While we all have the choice to either accept with grace or fight tooth and nail the things God has allowed us, it is my wish that you will gain confidence in the One who has given you this special, unexpected gift.

If you are not a parent of a child with special needs, I hope that you will gain greater understanding for those who have this special task as well as see how special families fulfill their role in the body of Christ. I believe there are many misconceptions about the child or adult with disabilities and their families—especially within the church—and I want to dispel some of those in this book. May you discover ways you can minister to a family who lives with a disability and how you can be ministered to by them.

Our job as parents of children with special needs, along with learning to care for our unexpected gifts, is to learn to trust the One who sent them. The world may not welcome our children with open arms, but God knows they belong here. Remember, the diagnosis of disability isn't the end of our life but the beginning of a new one. One that, in time, we will come to treasure.

CHAPTER 2

The Struggle of Diagnosis

How unsearchable [are the Lord's] judgments,
and his paths beyond tracing out!
"Who has known the mind of the Lord?
Or who has been his counselor?"
(Rom. 11:33b—34)

After we receive the news that our child has a disability, we often struggle with powerful emotions. Sometimes the diagnosis can be a relief; other times it may be a grave disappointment. And for some of us, it can be devastating. We handle test results and the consequential labels that are placed on our child according to the degree of disability and the way it specifically affects our child. If the prognosis is more hopeful, our feelings of disappointment may not be as overwhelming. And if our children are higher functioning, we may have greater confidence in ourselves and our ability to handle their special needs.

The journey to diagnosis puts us on an emotional roller coaster. Finding out precisely what is going on with our child can take an afternoon, a week, a month, or sometimes years. Sometimes we're never able to arrive at a complete diagnosis. Then what do we do?

In this chapter, I want to share with you the stories of some fellow parents and our experiences of getting, or trying to get, a diagnosis for our children. My hope is that you'll be able to see your own story in ours and not feel so alone. Then I'd like to take a look at what a diagnosis does and does not do for you and your child. For one thing, it doesn't give us all the answers—and understanding this can greatly help our peace of mind.

The Journey to Diagnosis

Few parents of children with special needs cannot recount to you the exact details of the moment they discovered their child would never be like the other kids. The color of the waiting room, the doctor's words, the way our child looked—these images have branded themselves on our minds. Though we share the searing of our memories, our personal roads to diagnosis are often quite different.

Are You Sure?

The diagnosis of autism for Ruth's son, Christopher, came during a time of family upheaval, including the death of a close family member. Suspecting that her son's high energy level and inability to stay on task might be symptoms of attention deficit disorder (ADD), she was shocked to find out that the local school district's preschool psychologist assessed him with autism. Though an earlier visit to the pediatrician had raised the suspicion of autism, chiefly because of Christopher's high-pitched scream, Ruth was still not prepared for the psychologist's official assessment.

"I was stunned," says Ruth, explaining,
I didn't know what to think. Being first-time parents, you
don't suspect anything—you just kind of go with the
flow. And none of the other pediatricians we had
taken him to over the course of his three years had said
anything to us about this, so we were surprised.

Sometimes the diagnosis of disability can blindside us— knock us flat. In an instant, the course of our lives takes an irrevocable turn. Getting up and moving forward draws on everything we have—and more. If only we'd had a little warning, just an inkling that something was wrong, perhaps that would have made it a little easier to bear.

Unfortunately, having a suspicion doesn't necessarily help—-especially when no one else seems to see what you see—as in Barb and Dave's case.

Doesn't Anyone See What We See?

It's strange, but sometimes we sense early on that something isn't quite right with our child, but other family members, friends, and even doctors insist that everything is just fine. Their resistance can make coping with the eventual diagnosis that much more difficult.

For Barb and Dave, the slow development of their youngest son caused concern—-but apparently only to them. Having two older children, Barb was familiar with what to expect in her child's growth, and she knew Brad was different. Barb recalls,

When Brad was three months old, it became obvious to me that he wasn't developing on schedule. He didn't hold toys, his muscle tone was limp, he was too compliant, he wasn't interested in his environment. And he wasn't using the left side of his body.

At that time, I brought my concerns to our pediatrician--who felt I was overreacting. We continued to watch and to grow more concerned with each month. When Brad was seven months old, he began having shaking episodes. We again brought these concerns to our pediatrician, and he again implied we were overreacting. But he did agree to refer us to a neurologist in our HMO.

We felt like no one was taking us seriously in the medical profession. We weren't sure if Brad had a brain tumor or what, and everyone was blowing us off! That was one of our most stressful times—begging for someone to help our son and take us seriously.

We decided to videotape Brad's seizures to bolster our credibility with the medical professionals. Finally, we were taken seriously, and our journey with the medical field began.

In the years that have followed, Dave and Barb have taken Brad to neurologists, metabolic geneticists, endocrinologists, general geneticists, neuro-ophthalmologists, ear-nose-and-throat specialists, orthopedists, and a host of other medical professionals. Their son has been diagnosed with thyroid problems, vision problems, cerebral palsy, seizures, severe mental retardation, and autism. These diagnoses definitely prove that they weren't overreacting, but they haven't provided complete clarity on what is going on with Brad either. Barb says,

> *At this point, they believe there is something that has caused all these issues, but they don't have a clue as to what. Brad has had numerous genetic tests that we were sure would render a definite diagnosis. It's hard to believe, but each time the tests come back negative, we have a sense of disappointment. The lack of clear diagnosis for everything has also left us feeling like we don't really belong to any one group of people who may be able to give us support.*

Not having a complete diagnosis clouds the future. If Brad's problems have a genetic origin, what are the implications for Barb and Dave's other two children? And really, how many of Brad's medical issues can be attributed to one root cause? "It would be so much easier," Barb confesses, "to have some kind of guideline in terms of what medical conditions can go with a diagnosis so we aren't always guessing."

Are We Bad Parents?

Julie and Tom were working overseas when they began noticing some behavior problems in their third child, Jason. Jason couldn't seem to sit still and seemed very impulsive. A visit to the pediatrician yielded a recommendation to see a psychoneurologist. Three months later, a diagnosis of attention deficit hyperactive disorder (ADHD) was given, which alleviated some of the feelings of guilt they had harbored for not being able to get their child to "behave properly."

Their next hurdle was getting their son the treatment he needed. "We were overseas," Julie explains, "and we had little support. As a result, we had to leave, resulting in a total job change." That was a hard decision to make, but Julie and Tom felt that finding good services for Jason was crucial. Back in the States, they pursued further evaluation and discovered that their son also had obsessive compulsive disorder (OCD), as well as related depression. Securing treatment has not been an easy task, but through God's grace, Jason has made progress.

Though Julie grieved and was discouraged knowing that "it was a tough road ahead," she was also relieved to finally know why their son acted the way he did. "We were comforted in the words spoken that Jason's condition wasn't our fault or our bad parenting."

When Does This Roller Coaster Stop?

Like many mothers of children with special needs, Gayle had a normal pregnancy. She had no indications that there were any problems, but her and her husband Ric's life took a turn on October 16, 1982. On this day, their daughter had her first grand mal seizure, as well as focal seizures. Baby Heather was flown to a children's hospital, where she underwent a CAT scan, an MRI, and a spinal tap. The doctors determined that she had a porencyphalic cyst (undeveloped brain matter) and cerebral palsy. Gayle remembers,

> At that time, they said she'd be OK cognitively but would have a limp, due to the brain damage done in utero, but they weren't sure. It would be a waiting game.
> I remember wondering what the future would hold for Heather after her initial seizure. I felt like I was holding my breath emotionally regarding the situation until I knew she would be OK. I think I was numb for the first year after she was diagnosed. Almost a year to the day, she had her second episode of seizures. So the emotions started again.

Between 1987 and 1991, the emotional roller coaster got wilder when Heather's seizures began coming more frequently, each one doing a little more damage to her brain. As Gayle recalls,

*The denial, disbelief, sadness, and numbness to life
continued through all of her seizing through 1991.
Heather would gain developmental milestones, and
then she would have an episode of seizures and lose all
the milestones she'd gained. And then the anger and
sadness would arise again.*

The doctors decided that Heather was a good candidate
for brain surgery, where the cystic portion of her brain would be
removed. While this surgery eliminated the seizures, it also
revealed that Heather's thinking had been affected far more
than her mobility, contrary to the initial prognosis.

Gayle and Ric had been through all the ups and downs of
Heather's spurts of growth and seizing setbacks; now they're on
that slow upward climb of adjusting to their daughter's new
needs. Gayle has observed that the longer you ride the roller
coaster, the more you learn how to get ready for the next high
point and the next low point, and the better you become at not
losing your emotional lunch.

Are We There Yet?

For my husband Jim and me, the roads to diagnoses for our
sons have been long and, at times, intertwined. While we deal
with different issues with each son, sometimes we are not sure
whether we are coping with the disability or just the whims of a
child. We have no other children who have developed
normally, so we are at a loss to gauge what is and isn't typical.
In addition, both of our sons are now considered high-
functioning, which causes some people to challenge their initial
diagnoses. For us, though, the memories of a challenging
development leave little question in our minds that our children
were created in a unique way.

Our oldest son Daniel was born after a difficult delivery with
several complications. We watched carefully as our son grew;
he was an active child, sleeping less than nine hours each day.
He was always a little bit late in reaching milestones, but he
always reached them within the acceptable window. He
seemed a bright and happy boy, and my worries ceased as
time went on.

A couple years later, our second son, Jonathan, was born. He was a good baby, an extremely strong, healthy boy who adhered to a strict schedule. But I was a little concerned that he didn't seem to be able to track objects properly, and he never seemed to look me in the eyes. We didn't suspect that anything was wrong until a "chance" appointment at a clinic a hundred miles from our home revealed our son's serious vision problems and a skull deformity.

I felt overwhelmingly sad as I looked down at my sweet, quiet baby. Outside the world went by as though nothing was wrong. But my world stopped.

Our three-month-old son underwent a craniectomy for a condition called craniosynostosis, which is a premature fusing of the skull that causes the growing brain to morph into an unusual shape. Thanks to the surgery, he was able to track objects for the first time; though he did have visual problems due to strabismus, or weakened eye muscles that caused one of his eyes to turn outward; and rotary nystagmus, the involuntary eye movements that would make his eyes look like they were wiggling like Jell-O. We were assured that there should be no problems with development, and we would just need to monitor his skull's regrowth and progress over the next year.

Daniel, on the other hand, though almost four years old by this point, still could not speak in a language we could understand, though he seemed to understand us. He was diagnosed by our local school district as having a central auditory processing disorder (CAPD), a condition where the hearing system is intact but the neural system has trouble deciphering the code of language. Physical therapies were also added for motor deficits.

After treatment for Daniel's CAPD began, I watched Jonathan even more carefully for signs of language delay. While he didn't seem to have trouble with language at this stage, we did have difficulty getting him to eat solid food. He was extremely tactilely defensive—texture of any type, whether it was touched by his hands or his mouth, was overwhelming to him. Having solid food touch his mouth caused projectile vomiting. So at his two-year checkup, we received exercises from a developmental therapist to eliminate the vomiting.

Expanding his extremely narrow range of food interests is still a part of our life, though.

And something else was happening to Jonathan. Despite his tactile defensiveness, he didn't seem to respond to pain. He would have tantrums (which were also mystifying) and bang his head, sometimes so violently we had to put our hands underneath to keep him from injuring himself. Then his language development changed—he preferred not to talk but would instead lead us by the hand when he wanted something. If he did speak, he simply repeated the last word of the question we asked him.

Not being able to communicate properly with my sons was probably the most heartbreaking thing for me. I often felt inadequate because I could not seem to meet their needs without lots of tears and screaming and wrong guesses. Sometimes I never did get it right. After bringing up these concerns to our pediatrician, we were referred to a pediatric neurologist. On March 21, 1995, a rainy and generally dismal day, we all trooped down to the neurologist's. Because Jonathan did display eye contact with his immediate family, the diagnosis for our younger son was that of an atypical type of autism. We were given a referral to our local regional center and sent home.

Because our pediatrician had said that this might be a possible diagnosis, we weren't completely shocked. Or at least we didn't think we were. Driving home, I convinced myself that our situation wasn't really that bad. I talked myself into thinking this way so I wouldn't lose myself in utter disappointment.

About a year after Jonathan's diagnosis of autism, we started the process of evaluating Daniel for attention problems. While his speech and language skills had improved, his inability to focus escalated. Rather haphazardly, in my opinion, we reached the diagnosis of ADD, possibly with hyperactivity.

Medication was offered as a tool to help Daniel sit in class. Medicating remains a rather controversial method of treatment, and I got my share of opinions from everyone. But I was glad that there was something we could try that might have rather dramatic results, though I was hesitant to give my child a stimulant. I was shocked at how well the medication worked. At least for a little while, we could settle into a routine of knowing our children's disabilities and their therapies. Now we at least were working with known entities. Or were we?

Four years after our world was blown apart by the startling diagnosis of autism, Jim and I once again found ourselves in a specialist's office. Daniel's current medication for ADHD seemed to have stopped working. We worried that, as he advanced through school, he would not be able to keep pace with his classmates despite his cognitive ability. What we found out that day, and confirmed at a later appointment, was that in addition to his learning disability and his ADHD, Daniel also had obsessive-compulsive behaviors (OCB) —he was a prisoner of his own repetitive thoughts and the need to "even things up." He also had Tourette's syndrome, a disorder characterized by seemingly meaningless vocal and motor tics or repetitions.

I guess I should have been stunned, but I wasn't. There was suddenly an explanation for certain behaviors I had simply attributed to the ADHD. I had learned my lesson from the last barn-burner diagnosis, autism. I was not going to saturate myself with too much information about Tourette's and OCB. Instead, I learned just enough to understand the medication choices and the general prognosis and left it at that. Not that it didn't come back to haunt me about six weeks later, when the pressure was on to inform the school of these new developments without scaring the pants off the educators. But I had learned earlier, when God had helped me to accept autism as part of our journey, that He knew what He was doing when He let another syndrome and another disorder invade our existence.

Several years, constant observation, and a variety of medications (some of which worked and some which didn't), led the educators dealing with Daniel to suggest that he, too, might have a higher form of autism. To be frank, I didn't really care what they called his syndrome as long as he received the proper supports in school. If it made it "better" to fill in a different box on the school's educational plan form, so be it. The problem was that Daniel now knew about autism was from watching his brother—and he hated that word and what it represented. It took some prayer and sensitivity to explain that this word, "autism" did not diminish his value as a human being.

What a Diagnosis Does and Doesn't Do

As parents of children with special needs, we have all had to come to terms with our children not being like other kids. As we have seen, sometimes the diagnosis of disability can be a great shock, a relief, or a continuing roller-coaster ride. Most of us spend a great deal of time, effort, and money to secure a diagnosis, and overall I think this is a good thing. However, I also believe that there is a definite downside to the diagnosis procedure. Let's take a look at both the ups and the downs.

The Upside

What do we hope a diagnosis will do? A diagnosis can help us understand why our children do what they do. It won't necessarily get rid of their behaviors or present a cure, but a diagnosis can point us in the right direction.

A diagnosis is simply a tool. It gives physicians and educators a starting point to provide appropriate therapies and medications. It gives us access to helpful literature and organizations, allowing us to connect and share support with others who may have a similar diagnosis. It opens the door to money provided by local agencies that serve the individual with disabilities.

Without a diagnosis, some of us play a pretend game, where we secretly hope that we will stumble upon the magic cure that will make our child instantly better. This is dangerous thinking, though, because then we never really know if the therapies and medications we're using are the most effective for our child.

In essence, a diagnosis provides us with a map so we know how to navigate in our children's world. It helps us know what we can do for our child, and it relieves us of what we cannot do.

The Downside

Some people spend a lot of money trying to get a diagnosis, while others spend a lot of money trying to shake one. For those who have a diagnosis, it can feel like a sticky label you can't peel off. When you look at it, it helps explain the "ingredients" inside your child. But sometimes you don't want people to see the ingredients. The label might not be accurate, it might not be appropriate, and it might scare people.

When I first looked at the definition of autism, it depressed me beyond measure. Early literature written on the subject of autism seemed to suggest that my younger son's condition was hopeless. Lifelong and not curable were two phrases I did not enjoy seeing in the same sentence. Of course, a developmental disability is lifelong, but it looks so nasty to see it stated in print. But not curable is not the same as "not treatable," and autism is treatable. It's just not known how treatable it is for each individual child. Every child responds differently to therapies, and every child with autism is often affected differently. There is no way of knowing what a diagnosis portends for the future. But it often feels like the stroke of doom.

In addition, a possible misdiagnosis, or a missed diagnosis, is heartbreaking. Though we thought we already knew the extent of our older son's problems, we later learned more—that he had Tourette's syndrome. We had been using a certain stimulant for his ADHD that, to our horror, actually made the tics of Tourette's worse. How foolish we felt, even though we were doing the best with the knowledge we had. Do we still know everything there is to know about our son in terms of diagnosis? We're not sure, and this raises a disturbing question: If my child now has a new diagnosis, does that mean he has changed? Did he "catch" a different disability? Or did we mess up?

In our case, our older son's later and more severe diagnosis of autism brought the painful realization that he has always had it and we have always missed it. I can't help feeling that we as his parents, his doctors, and his school officials have failed him for the last decade of his life. If he does indeed have autism, a syndrome that can encompass the ADHD, obsessive-compulsive behaviors, Tourette's, and various learning disabilities, then have we squandered his childhood on useless therapies and denied him the services he qualifies for? His younger brother got what he needed and has flourished. Have we blown it for our older son?

These are hard things to think about. But there is no way to go back now. We did the best we could with the information we had at the time.

Another down side is when we're pressured to arrive at a certain diagnosis in order to get more services for our children, such as extra classroom help. We certainly want our children to get all the help they need, but do we want to glue a label on them—a label that may be worse than what they actually have—that they'll never be able to get off?

Beyond Diagnosis

I think the most important thing to remember when going through this discovery process is that a diagnosis is not the sum total of who our children are. A diagnosis doesn't really change our child in any way. It doesn't change their interests, their likes and dislikes, their sense of humor, their unique personalities. A diagnosis simply provides clues about how to help our kids, but it doesn't define them.

Your children, and my children, are bigger than their diagnoses—they are so much more than a list of symptoms and disorders! They, too, have been made in God's image, have been gifted by Him, and have eternal souls.

A diagnosis may change the way we express love to our children so that they can receive it . . . but it never changes our love for them, and their need for our love, any more than our human "disabilities" change God's love for us:

The Lord is gracious and compassionate,
slow to anger and rich in love.
The Lord is good to all;
he has compassion on all he has made. . . .
The Lord is faithful to all his promises
and loving toward all he has made.
The Lord upholds all those who fall
and lifts up all who are bowed down.
(Ps. 145:8—9, 13b—14)

I have loved you with an everlasting love. (Jer. 31:3)

God demonstrates his own love for us in this: While we
were still sinners, Christ died for us. (Rom. 5:8)

His love endures forever. (Ps. 136:1b)

CHAPTER 3

Whose Fault Is This?

Looking for Someone to Blame

*"Rabbi, who sinned, this man or his parents, that he
was born blind?" "Neither this man nor his parents
sinned," said Jesus, "but this happened so that the
work of God might be displayed in his life."*
(JOHN 9:2—3)

"Did you have a difficult pregnancy?" "Did you have a
traumatic birth?" "Does anyone in your family have a similar
disability?" "Did you drink or take drugs during your
pregnancy?" I am sure that you have been subjected to this
barrage of questions by medical professionals, friends or
acquaintances, or even members of your own family. Everyone
wants to know why this happened, what caused this child to
have these disabilities—or as the disciples asked, "Who sinned?"
    And you know what? At some level, we want to know too.
    When I meet with other moms of children with special needs,
we often recount to each other our child's birth story or the early
days of his or her development. We examine every nuance of a
doctor's comment, recite clues we should have picked up on
about our child's latent diagnosis, and play the "if only I knew
then what I know now" game. We feel compelled to
understand why things happened as they did . . . as if knowing

21

this meant that somehow we could go back and erase the disability from our child's life.

Assigning responsibility can be our way of finding some control in a situation that feels completely out of control. Maybe if we knew who or what caused this, we could make sure it would never happen again.

But even if we did know exactly when and how the damage to our child's brain and body occurred, what could we do then? We can't go back in time, we can't undo what's been done, and we may not even be able to prevent it from happening again.

Unfortunately, rational thought doesn't always stop us from entering the endless maze of blame. Let's look at how we rightly or wrongly blame ourselves, others, and even God and figure out a way to move beyond blame's imprisoning hold.

When We Know What Happened

Sometimes we do know what "bad thing" happened to bring about our child's disability. The doctor may have made mistakes during delivery. Someone may have failed to watch the baby properly. The drunk driver who crashed into our car left our child with a brain injury. Our spouse may have abused our child.

Or we may have done it ourselves.

Maybe we didn't take care of ourselves during pregnancy the way we should have. Maybe we didn't bother with prenatal vitamins or regular checkups. Maybe we drank or took drugs. Maybe we didn't watch the baby properly. Maybe we crashed the car. Maybe we struck our child and gave her brain damage.

Whether accidental or intentional, when we know what happened, we're often flooded with helplessness, anger at the perpetrator, guilt for not protecting our child better, or shame for hurting our child ourselves. Every day, as we struggle to raise a child with special needs, we face the visible reminder of our own or someone else's carelessness, neglect, ineptitude, or malice.

How do we find our way out of this hellish turmoil? How do we move through the rage of blame to acceptance and peace? Heaven knows we have more than enough tumultuous emotions to deal with in raising a child with special needs—we really can't afford to heap on more guilt, anger, or shame.

I think the only course God leaves open to us is the steep, narrow path of forgiveness. I say steep because it's neither easy nor immediate. Forgiveness is not saying that something wrong is not wrong, that something bad is OK. Forgiving is not excusing the inexcusable or smoothing over the rough edges of sin. As Lewis Smedes writes,

> *Forgiving comes equipped with the toughness of realism. To be able to forgive we must have the guts to look hard at the wrongness, the horridness, the sheer wickedness of what somebody did to us. We cannot camouflage; we cannot excuse; we cannot ignore. We eye the evil face to face and we call it what it is. Only realists can be forgivers.*[1]

The rage we feel from being wronged can sometimes motivate us to be forceful advocates for our special child. But a life of rage is not what God wants for us. Instead, He wants us to do the unnatural:

> *"When you stand praying, if you hold anything against anyone, forgive him, so that your Father in heaven may forgive you your sins." (Mark 11:25—26)*

These words are easy to read but so hard to live. And they don't feel right to us, do they? Those who are wronged are obligated to forgive, and if they don't, they are the ones who will be penalized? It seems entirely unfair. Yet that's the nature of grace: giving people (including ourselves) not what they deserve but what they need. This is what Christ did for us: "When we were God's enemies, we were reconciled to him through the death of his Son. . . . It is by grace you have been saved" (Rom. 5:10; Eph. 2:5).

Now, unless we are naturally forgiving people, learning to forgive ourselves or the person who wounded our child is a process that may require outside help. For starters, I would recommend Smedes' book <u>Forgive and Forget: Healing the Hurts We Don't Deserve</u>. He's very honest about what forgiveness is and isn't, and he is realistic about the process while

23

being centered in the Bible's teaching. A pastor, a counselor, or a Bible study may also be a good place to learn how to follow Christ's command to forgive. And connecting with other individuals who have had to learn the art of forgiveness, who understand your struggles and your reluctance to grant grace, can be crucial to your journey. Above all, pray that God will grant you the grace to begin to forgive others—as well as yourself.

Remember, blame cannot change the reality we have to deal with in the present; it only makes our journey that much harder.

When We Don't Know What Happened

Blame is hard enough to live with when we can point our finger at a real person, but when we don't know what caused our child's disability, we tend to look everywhere for someone to accuse—no matter how improbable.

Not long ago, my husband, Jim, and I decided to consult an expert in ADHD regarding our son Daniel. Because he hadn't been assessed in a while, and we wanted to explore other options for medications, we made an appointment at a local, well-respected medical center. In preparation, I was required to fill out close to one hundred pages of questions. Emotions I thought I had buried long ago resurfaced, especially as I reviewed my old paperwork. In looking through all the reports we had collected over the years, I was struck by how disjointed—and in some cases, incorrect—many of the earlier reports had been. And blame crept in: What was I thinking not to have argued these assessments? How could I not have been aware of the severity of Daniel's language disorder? How could all those clinicians and therapists not have noticed? Did we get the proper treatments? Did we miss something? Are we missing something now? I really didn't have any answers to these gnawing questions.

The information the doctor wanted relating to Daniel's birth and infancy was the most disturbing to fill out. What started as a routine labor ended up with me on oxygen "for the baby" and a prolonged, painful delivery. Epidurals were not routinely authorized by my HMO, and it occurred to me on the delivery table that Eve had committed one onerous deed to have inflicted womankind with "greatly multiplied" pain in childbirth! Daniel was born in a transverse position (sideways), and only after manual palpation—which means that the midwife, Jim, and two nurses squeezed Daniel out like toothpaste out of a tube.

Nobody in the delivery room was in good shape after the birth. Daniel's Apgar score was a five, with the high being ten. Five means "needs resuscitation." That would explain why he was blue and made no noise for some time and why the midwife panicked and yelled for one of the nurses to get a doctor now! When I asked, "What's wrong with the baby?" no one would answer me. When I asked Jim, he grabbed my hand and simply said, "God is in control." One of the nurses eventually found a heartbeat, and by the time the doctor arrived, Daniel was breathing.

These pictures in my mind made me nervous all the first year of his life. Did he get enough oxygen at birth? Is he going to have problems because of his rough start? He had a poor sucking reflex, so I couldn't feed him, and our HMO had not yet hired a lactation consultant to help with the problem. None of the nurses had been able to help me breast-feed him either, but they sent us home anyway. I tried in desperation; but I finally gave up and switched to bottles. This led to guilt for not being "a real mother" who "cared enough" to breast-feed her baby. Every time I read that infants who were nursed were healthier and had higher IQs, I felt like a bad mom. Every time another mother clicked her tongue in shame when she heard I didn't breast-feed my baby, I felt like a bad woman. And I already felt like a bad woman because I believed I had nearly killed my baby on the delivery table.

Then, when we discovered that Daniel had some delays, I couldn't help but think that if I had demanded better health care, he wouldn't need the extra help. As I waded through a hundred memories while I filled out the hundred pages of the questionnaire, more questions swirled through my mind, hurling me down in a spiral of blame: What if I had demanded a C-section? What if I had insisted on help in feeding Daniel? What if I had sought help for his language delay sooner? What if I didn't talk so fast myself—would Daniel have understood language better? I am his chief advocate——what if his problems are entirely my fault?

Have you beat yourself up with questions like these? If so, you're certainly not alone. In my church group for moms with kids who have special needs, we all ask these questions. We wonder about illnesses we or our children have had. We wonder if we should have taken those antibiotics while pregnant or nursing. We wonder if our doctors are competent. We wonder if we should have had genetic counseling——then we wonder what we would have done with that information. On and on it goes, wondering, what-iffing, blaming anything we can think of.

But you know, even if we knew the cause or causes, we still could not go back and change anything. All our mental gymnastics profit us nothing, because our circumstances haven't changed. Maybe in all our theorizing, we are looking for a hint of purpose in that which seems purposeless. We want to know a reason for our child's and our own pain. We want to know why.

But will we ever know why on this earth? Most likely, the answer is no. The explanation for why our children are the way they are will probably remain a mystery for all our lifetime. What we need to do, then, is train ourselves to stop asking why, to stop seeking someone to blame (including ourselves), to stop wasting our energy trying to "unscrew the inscrutable" and save our resources for our child's and our family's needs. When the temptation to brood over why comes along, first, recognize what is happening——let the word why be a tip-off that you're probably entering a dark cavern that's easy to get lost in. Then, make a conscious, deliberate decision to not go there. Stay in the reality of the present instead of fantasizing about the past. You may have to make this decision again and again, but with practice, you can avoid this painful pitfall.

Some of us don't struggle so much with looking back as with looking up——our whys aren't directed at ourselves but at God. Unfortunately, in the Christian community, being upset with God is not often warmly welcomed. However, those feelings and thoughts are real, and they need to be brought out into the open if we're going to get through——and beyond——them.

Why Did God Let This Happen?

Now that we have in our child a living, breathing example that we are not in control of much, our faith searches for who is in control. Was God looking the other way when our child became disabled? Or—a thought that is sometimes more troubling—-was He not looking the other way? Did He deliberately, knowingly allow this to happen?

All of our lessons about the character of God come into question in light of our present situation. We wonder what kind of God would allow a small child to suffer. Is He punishing us or our child? And if so, why? A newborn baby has not committed any sin yet that would merit punishment, and since we're forgiven believers, hasn't Christ borne the punishment for our sins already anyway? If God is loving, why does He let us hurt? If God is omnipotent, why doesn't He do something to help our child and us? If God is good, what possible reason could He have for allowing this "bad" thing?

We may know the proper Sunday school answers to these questions, but they don't often satisfy the needs of our hearts as we ponder our situation and the future. The One we need most is the One we don't trust right now, because we just don't understand Him.

Our Rules

Many of us, despite knowing better, believe down deep that if we do good things and serve God well, then only good things will follow us all the days of our life. And if we do bad things and ignore God, then we get what's coming to us. This cause-and-effect thinking gives us the illusion of safety—but that's all it is, an illusion. Good people die young after a painful fight against cancer, and bad people live comfortably into old age. Honest people struggle to make a living, while dishonest people grow rich and live in luxury. Kind people get stepped on, yet ruthless people make it to the top. Our belief, however, stubbornly persists, and when painful or difficult things happen to us—good people—we blame God and call Him unfair.

Jesus, however, challenges our thinking. Take a look at some of the things He taught:

"[The Father] causes his sun to rise on the evil and the good, and sends rain on the righteous and the unrighteous." (Matt. 5:45)

Now there were some present at that time who told Jesus about the Galileans whose blood Pilate had mixed with their sacrifices. Jesus answered, "Do you think that these Galileans were worse sinners than all the other Galileans because they suffered this way? I tell you, no! But unless you repent, you too will all perish. Or those eighteen who died when the tower in Siloam fell on them—do you think they were more guilty than all the others living in Jerusalem? I tell you, no! But unless you repent, you will all perish." (Luke 13:1—5)

The passage from Matthew shows us that good things happen to the good and the bad—God is generous and merciful. But Luke reveals that bad things happen to people who are no worse than any of the rest of us—and Jesus directs us to deal with our own sins rather than take false comfort from the fate of others.

We aren't unique in believing in a cause-and-effect world. Throughout history, disability was seen as the visible marker of hidden sin. The person with a disability or serious illness was an outcast, often left to beg at the city gates. But Jesus tells us that disability and sin are not necessarily linked at all:

As he went along, he saw a man blind from birth. His disciples asked him, "Rabbi, who sinned, this man or his parents, that he was born blind?"

"Neither this man nor his parents sinned," said Jesus, "but this happened so that the work of God might be displayed in his life." (John 9:1—3)

OK, Jesus may have convinced us that pain and suffering may not be caused by what we do or don't do, and that God has a greater purpose in it. But where does that leave us? The blind man in John would be healed, but our children remain in their disabilities. What work of God is being displayed in their lives? And besides, what kind of God deliberately allows a baby's body or mind to form abnormally? This still doesn't seem fair, does it? What right does God have to mess with our lives like this?

God's Rule

God has a sovereign right to shape our lives in whatever fashion He wishes.

Now there's a truth that sticks in our throats like a small, sharp bone. And boy, do we have trouble swallowing it, let alone digesting it!

Have you ever grappled with the picture of God that the book of Job provides? In the first chapter, the heavenly hosts converge, and Satan shows up among them. God questions the Prince of Darkness:

"Where have you come from?"
Satan answered the Lord, "From roaming through the earth and going back and forth in it." (Job 1:7)

The Lord then points Job out to Satan as a fine example of a servant of God. But Satan has the gall to mock God, saying that of course Job serves Him because the Lord gives him everything! Then Satan challenges the Lord:

"But stretch out your hand and strike everything he has, and he will surely curse you to your face." (v. 11)

Incredibly, the Lord takes up this challenge, but He adds one caveat:

"Very well, then, everything he has is in your hands, but on the man himself do not lay a finger." (v. 12)

God allowed Satan to wound His servant. God allowed the Evil One to wreak destruction in Job's life.

Certainly, Satan bears responsibility for the cruel harm he inflicts on people. Even my young son Daniel can see that. When we were going to a picnic for families who had a member with special needs, I wanted to prepare him for what he would see. As I explained that some of the kids had seizures and some had had strokes, he looked at me solemnly and said, "Mom, Satan does really bad things." Yes, he does. What Satan does comes from within his own corrupt mind.

But he can't touch us without God's permission.

To some, the idea that a loving, good God would allow Satan to wound people seems contradictory, if not heretical. To get around this, some have argued that God is not behind our wounding but our sin nature causes our woundedness. To a certain extent, this is true. We are personally responsible for the way our words and actions hurt others. However, since we all have a sin nature (see Ps. 51:5), we should each then have profound pain from disease, disability, or death. Yet many somehow manage to miss the major hurts of life—chronic illness, disability, divorce—while others are challenged by them all.

It doesn't seem fair that some folks run through life seemingly unscathed and others have more than their share of heartache. When we were so careful during pregnancy to take good prenatal care, why did our child end up with a birth defect? Why didn't the lady down the street, who smoked and occasionally drank during her pregnancy, have a child with a disability? The line between personal responsibility and the will of God becomes so easily confused. And it's so hard to understand that the God who gave His Son's life for us and has stored up all the treasure of heaven for us also can and does wound us.

Look at what the Lord says of Himself in His Word:

"Who gave man his mouth? Who makes him deaf or mute? Who gives him sight or makes him blind? Is it not I, the Lord?" (Exod. 4:11)

"See now that I myself am He!
There is no god besides me.
I put to death and I bring to life,
I have wounded and I will heal,
and no one can deliver out of my hand." (Deut. 32:39)
"I am the LORD, and there is no other.
I form the light and create darkness,
I bring prosperity and create disaster;
I, the LORD, do all these things." (Isa. 45:6b—7)

If we believe that God is all-powerful, then He really does have the power even to wound. And if we believe He is sovereign, then He must be sovereign over even those things we feel He has overlooked.

In their book <u>When God Weeps</u>, Joni Eareckson Tada and Steven Estes tackle the same questions about God's sovereignty, our personal responsibility, and Satan's influence:

> God doesn't just watch [harm] happen—he lets it happen. What is accidental from our perspective was specifically allowed by God. He who holds all things together must sustain the very molecules of the brick and axehead as they fly toward their mark (Colossians 1:17). His allowing is not something offhanded or casual.
>
> . . . Evil can only raise its head where God deliberately backs away—always for reasons that are specific, wise, and good, but often hidden during this present life. . . .
>
> . . . God sees the evil already there and steers it to serve his good purposes and not merely Satan's viperous ones. It's as if he says, "So you want to sin? Go ahead—but I'll make sure you sin in a way that ultimately furthers my ends even while you're shaking your fist in my face." This is why we can accept troubles as ultimately from God even when the most dreadful people deliver them.[2]

Without God in absolute control, the harm we experience now would be far worse.

Finding Our Way with God

If we ever pictured God as a Benevolent Nanny whose job was to soothe our ruffled feathers, our child's disability put that to rest. As the Lord says in Isaiah, "Surely, as I have planned, so it will be, and as I have purposed, so it will stand" (Isa. 14:24). Our child's disability was not an accident or a punishment; it's just part of God's inscrutable plan.

Our job, then, is to stop asking why and to start turning to Him to teach us how. We need to learn to trust that He knows what

He's doing, that He really does love us, and that He will uphold us in our pain. We need to release our blame and our anger— stop hating the life He has given us. As Lewis Smedes observes, "Hating God's most precious gift [life] is a believer's sneaky way to hate God."[3]

Does trust come easily? It hasn't for me. By nature, I'm not a trusting person. I tend to question people's motives and doubt that they have my best interests at heart. I fear being duped, tricked, or betrayed, so I hold back, reluctant to give much of myself and be vulnerable.

Yet giving our entire selves is precisely what God asks us to do. Not only does He ask us to give ourselves away, but He asks us to believe that it is for our own good. And He provides little more instruction than "Trust me." What do we do with this?

I have found that I should treat this command like all other scriptural commands—namely, just do it, with His help. It's a matter of decision:

• I decide, contrary to my feelings, to believe God loves me.

• I decide to believe that He knows more than I do and is able to guide me to better decisions than I could concoct myself.

• I decide to give all my fears and hurts and anger to Him and let Him deal with them.

• I decide, since God plans all the details of my life, to let Him deal with all the details of my life.

This is a conscious act of the will—I practice this because trusting does not come easily to me. Nor does it feel natural. But playing a new sport or learning a new musical instrument doesn't feel natural either. We may get sore moving muscles we normally don't use or mind-boggled by the new language of musical notes. But if we practice, over time the sport or instrument becomes an extension of ourselves.

Is practicing fun? Even some professionals don't like to practice. Famed cellist Yo Yo Ma revealed in an interview that the thing he hates most about playing the cello is the practicing.

But he practices whether he wants to or not, because he knows that if he doesn't, he will not be able to master the music.

It's the same for us. Learning to trust God does not feel natural, but if we practice it diligently, it will come more easily. We will probably never master it; I think we will always have to practice trusting. Even if we recall all the times God has carried us through tough times, we'll probably still wonder, "What if He doesn't do it this time?" Then we have to tell ourselves, "He will." Not because we think He will or hope He will, but simply because He will. Practice thinking about all the ways He takes care of you. Practice thinking about how much He thinks about you. Practice thinking about how great it's going to be when you finally get to ask Him all your questions. Because one day, you will!

Sometimes, when I find myself wandering in a morass of angst, I do a couple of things. I remind myself that I can't think about two things at the same time, so I choose to think about the good. And I remind myself that God didn't make any mistakes when He allowed the circumstances of my life. I need to trust Him on that, because if I don't, I will become bitter. God chose this life for me knowing my personality, skills, and desires. I don't understand this by a long shot, so I trust this by a sheer act of will. I would not have chosen me for the job of parenting two boys with special needs, but God did. I have to trust that one day He will reveal why He chose me and lean on Him in the meantime.

Concluding Thoughts

After a trial in which we have emerged victorious, we often say that God seems bigger. But He is always big, and He always was, is, and will be a loving God. We as parents of children with special needs have the opportunity to trust in this big God, even though we may not see the end to our trial or the purpose in it here on earth. Truly, God is beyond all that we can imagine with our finite brains:

Though he brings grief, he will show compassion,
so great is his unfailing love.

For he does not willingly bring affliction
or grief to the children of men. (Lam. 3:32—33)

It's a scary thing to do, to trust a God who sees fit to place what seems like an impossible task on weak, fallible people. It hasn't been easy for me to trust a God who both wounds and heals. But in order to bind our wounds, He requires our trust and obedience. When we are ready—and He never hurries the process—the Great Physician has an excellent wound-care program. And He'll bring us to the place where we can echo the words of the psalmist:

We went through fire and water,
but you brought us to a place of abundance.
(Ps.66:12b)

CHAPTER 4

The Crucible of Shock, Denial, and Grief

The Lord is close to the brokenhearted
and saves those who are crushed in spirit.
(Ps. 34:18)

The common threads of multicolored emotions that weave through a life of disability so often feel like they are entangling our hearts, minds, and faith. Did you ever think you had so many feelings or that they ran so deep? Our child's disabilities bring to the surface a multitude of troubling emotions—or rather, seem to toss us down into a dark, bottomless pit.

Why do we feel so threatened by these movements of our hearts? Because some of the waves of pain they bring feel like they will drown us. Our feelings really feel that big. But there is something worse: the belief that it's not "Christian" to have deep struggles of the heart. What is it that swells the billows of shock, denial, grief, anger, and fear? It is shame—and there is a lot of it. We feel shame for not being able to handle things better, or for being negative. There is shame for feeling weak, and shame over wrestling with what the Lord has given us. Mostly, there is shame for feeling like this about our own child.

What do people do when they are ashamed? As Adam and Eve showed us, they hide (see Gen. 3:8—10). When we don't want others to see our distress, we sometimes mask our concerns about our child and about our own lives. We nod along with the Bible verses some helpful soul quotes to us, but inside we remain troubled or even seethe with resentment. Or maybe we don't want to know what feelings are roiling around inside of us, so we pretend they aren't there. We can become so expert at this that we even think we can hide our hearts from the Lord.

But we can't hide from God—and He doesn't want us to. In this chapter and the next two, let's be honest about the feelings many of us encounter. I say "many of us" because not everyone struggles with the same emotions or feels them to the same degree. Whatever we do feel, though, we need to know that we can take it to the Lord. We can be fearful and still trust Him. We can be angry and still love Him. We can feel the whole range of our feelings and still be good parents and live lives that are pleasing to the Lord. It's not easy—God doesn't offer "one-prayer fixes." But He promises to stay right beside us, guiding us every step of the way.

Shock and Denial

Even though many parents of children with disabilities often suspect something is wrong with their child's development, it is still a shock to hear a professional say it out loud. We resist the diagnosis sometimes because of our misconceptions about the characteristics of a certain disability; our child doesn't behave in those ways, so how could he or she have that diagnosis?

If symptoms come on suddenly, like seizures, we're often in shock because the timing seems all wrong. We had planned to go to the market, but we ended up in the emergency room. This can't be happening to our child! This isn't what we envisioned for our lives. Suddenly, it seems like we are living someone else's version of our life. Things take on a strange dreamlike quality, where everything looks, smells, and sounds exaggerated. We hear what the professionals are saying, but it doesn't add up. When we get home, everything that was once familiar looks and feels different. We expect to wake up any moment but are disappointed to find that we aren't sleeping. We keep reading the literature or the doctor's notes, hoping to find the one loophole to release us from this diagnosis. The doctor must have missed something.

In my experience, I thought I skipped denial and went directly to shock. This has been true about my response to all the diagnoses our sons have received over the years. I had suspected—-or more likely, God had planted seeds of suspicion—that something wasn't quite right with our sons' development. So it wasn't a big surprise to hear a clinician confirm a developmental delay and a disability. What did shock me was what the disabilities were. Autism? Tourette's syndrome? What—autism again? I had never even imagined having a child, much less two children, with such labels.

Each time I left a neurologist's office with a new name for what ailed my children, I didn't react. I would say, "Aha, so that's what it is!" And then, "Well, the doctor didn't seem too alarmed. I'm sure it's no big deal." I kept waiting for a torrent of tears, but at first it didn't come. What I did do was read way too many books and hit way too many websites on the internet. My plan to keep my feelings at bay was to completely immerse myself in an overload of information about my sons' disabilities. But reading about their futures was shocking, though I did a good job of denying it.

Parents aren't the only ones who float down the river of denial. Family members, friends, and acquaintances, in an effort to comfort us, often make comments that dismiss the neurologist's claims: "Are you sure? She seems fine to me." "Oh, you know how kids develop at different rates; he'll catch up!" "What he needs is a little discipline, that's all!" "Boys are just late talkers, don't you know?" These comments, however, come across more like "Don't worry, be happy." Instead of walking the trail of pain with us, these people stand far-off and call us to a dead end of false hope. Although is it not what they intended, this is the effect they have.

Other people will try to jolly us out of our concerns by engaging in what I call a "reverse contest." In this situation, a friend or relative tries to convince us that her non-disabled child has some "odd quirks" just like our child. Her child doesn't eat food either, she says. You try to explain how pronounced your child's problem is: the narrow range of food he'll eat, the vomiting, the trips to the occupational therapist. But she insists that her child hates food too. And she'll tell you about all the foods her child won't eat—except for the one he's wolfing down at the moment. If only my child had such a "problem," you think! You begin to protest again but soon realize that it is pointless to labor the point any further.

We even play "reverse contest" with other parents of children with special needs, trying to convince them that our child is more disabled than theirs. In this case, we end up denigrating our children and their capabilities, and again, everyone loses.

Denial is indeed a way of coping with pain when we aren't ready to accept it. But it is a stage we must move through if we're going to help our children. And regarding other people's responses, as much as we would like others to recognize the challenges we face, we can't always count on them. But the Lord truly knows and understands what our days hold, and we can count on Him.

Grief

Once the shock and denial of diagnosis wear off, whatever was pushed down inside our heads and hearts comes out— sometimes with a vengeance. It can really feel horrid, and we'll long for the days when numbness was our companion. We can't seem to deal with just one emotion; they get all mixed up with other emotions that have nothing to do with our child's disability. We'll have days when we are unsure what we're feeling and why we're feeling it. Are we sad? Are we angry? Are we scared? Why now? How can we explain to others how we feel when we don't even know ourselves? This stage can feel isolating, like we're turned inside out, unable to articulate it, and with no idea of how to fix it. Welcome to grief.

What Are We Grieving?

Webster's New World Dictionary defines grief as "intense emotional suffering caused by loss, disaster, misfortune, etc.; acute sorrow; deep sadness." Are we dealing with loss? Yes, in a way, we are. Our children haven't died, but our dreams for our life and for theirs have. It may seem strange, but we really mourn deeply the loss of our dreams.

In his book A <u>Grace Disguised</u>, Gerald Sittser describes the effects that loss can have—whether it's the death of a loved one, the loss of a job, the end of a marriage, or lost hopes and dreams:

> Loss creates a barren present, as if one were sailing on a vast sea of nothingness. Those who suffer loss live suspended between a past for which they long and a future for which they hope. They want to return to the harbor of the familiar past and recover what was lost— good health, happy relationships, a secure job. Or they want to sail on and discover a meaningful future that promises to bring them life again—successful surgery, a second marriage, a better job. Instead, they find themselves living in a barren present that is empty of meaning. Memories of the past only remind them of what they have lost; hope for the future only taunts them with an unknown too remote even to imagine.[1]

Loss is accompanied by feelings of acute and deep sadness. We grieve over all that our children may never get to do. We are sad that they may never have friends, live independently, get married, or have children. We mourn over the interruption of the natural order of things—children growing and maturing to take their place in the world and possibly care for us as we age. We don't expect to take care of our children all our lives. So for the limits placed both on their lives and ours, we grieve.

In my initial grieving over the diagnoses of my sons, the feeling of sadness seemed to turn me inside out. I tried to anchor myself in Scriptures such as Psalm 30:5: "Weeping may remain for a night, but rejoicing comes in the morning." I understood this verse, but I wondered when (or if?) the morning would come. I have never liked to cry, but once I get going, I can do it really well. I'll try with all my power to not cry in front of anyone, but when night comes and everyone is asleep, I can release the sobs of my heart. I have the telltale puffy eyes and a pounding headache the next morning; but even though I hate to weep, I know that somewhere, sometime, the tears must be spilled.

I've also learned to weep and do simple chores around the house at the same time. I like to call it emotional multitasking—-feeling awful yet still accomplishing menial jobs. I might as well be productive while I'm crying! It doesn't matter if I cry as I wash dishes or clean the kitchen. The tears can always be wiped off the counter or the stove.

But I've also learned to set a limit on the tears. I can cry when I clean, but I'd better stop before I answer the phone or go to the store. I can weep when my child's back is turned, but I'd better pull it together when he turns around. My child doesn't need the additional burden of my sadness. And I remember that one day God will personally wipe away all the tears that made my eyes red and puffy and my head ache. I can scarcely imagine what that day will be like.

My sadness does not always seem to be just for my children; it is also for the other children I know whose disabilities were more profound. I think about all the indignities and rejections they will encounter as life goes on and how none of it is their fault. But where my sons were concerned, I have struggled with feeling at fault because their particular disabilities are thought to have a genetic basis—from my DNA. I have grieved over that too.

Sadness over disability can also bring to the surface long-lost feelings that are unrelated to the present situation. This can be terribly confusing. Not only will we cry for our own and others' children, but we'll sometimes cry for every loss we've ever encountered. We may think about pets that ran away, friends who moved or changed interests, boyfriends or girlfriends who rejected us, all the dances we never went to. These things have nothing whatsoever to do with the situation at hand, but they're part of the collective pool of our emotional pain. So they will pop into our heads, unbidden, and mingle with our current sadness. And often they'll feel like they are adding fuel to an already blazing fire.

The Varied Faces of Grief

It's helpful to know that grief's first appearance often comes in a show of force. After that, it visits us in a variety of guises. C. S. Lewis opens his book A <u>Grief Observed</u> by telling of his surprise at how grief felt:

*No one ever told me that grief felt so like fear. I am
not afraid, but the sensation is like being afraid. The
same fluttering in the stomach, the same restlessness,
the yawning. I keep on swallowing.*
*At other times it feels like being mildly drunk, or
concussed. There is a sort of invisible blanket between
the world and me. I find it hard to take in what anyone
says. Or perhaps, hard to want to take it in. . .*
*And no one ever told me about the laziness of grief.
Except at my job—where the machine seems to run on
much as usual—I loathe the slightest effort.*[2]

Grief can also feel as if it is smothering us. It rides on our
backs all day and goes to bed with us. When we struggle to
wake up in the morning, it's sitting on top of our heads. We can't
quite see it in the dark, but then we finally make out its shape.
Frankly, we wish it would just leave us alone so we can get to the
business at hand. We don't have time for grief, and we don't
want to bog anyone else down with it either. We ask the Lord to
release us from it and are bitterly disappointed to find that grief
stays anyway. Maybe we try to run back to denial to see if we
can ditch grief there. But it always stands at the door, like a
pushy salesman, not letting us escape.

An important aspect of grief that we need to realize is that
each person's experience of it is unique. Some people are
overwhelmed with grief; others don't feel it that much. There is
no "right" way to grieve.

For example, Claudia and John, who had waited more than
a decade to conceive a child, finally had a son, David.
Unfortunately, he failed to thrive after several weeks, and a
number of other problems became apparent: his eyes turned
inward and moved involuntarily, he developed asthmatic
bronchitis, and he had developmental delays. In kindergarten,
he was diagnosed with Asperger's syndrome, which is on the
autism spectrum. How did Claudia cope with all of this? She
never feared anything but simply trusted that the Lord knew
what He was doing. When asked about her feelings regarding
the journey she travels with her son, she turns to Job 2:10: "Shall
we accept good from God, and not trouble?" She is a unique

person, certainly; one who can deal calmly with whatever is put in front of her.

Not all of us are like this, though. More likely, we will struggle and our situation may have dramatic effects on our lives. In Kay's case, a routine amniocentesis in her fifth month of pregnancy revealed her son to have Down syndrome. Here's how she described her feelings:

> *I love children . . . and my first two kids are adopted. So after seventeen years of marriage and pregnant for the first time, it was a very special time for our family. But when I found this out, I felt like I was in a car approaching a block wall at high speed. I was terrified, more than I can express. Nights I lay sleepless, heart pounding, shaking.*

Her son Michael developed congestive heart problems, feeding problems, multiple seizures, and deafness. The strain of many hospital stays and long hours of care drained her and her husband of energy needed to sustain their marriage, and they divorced. This is not uncommon in families who care for children with special needs. The relentless demands and the strong and sometimes conflicting emotions can set two partners against each other instead of drawing them together for mutual support.

I confess that in my own experience, I wondered about my husband's reaction to our sons' diagnoses. While I was completely surprised by the depth of my grief, Jim seemed not to bat an eye. I would ask him, "Doesn't our situation upset you?" And he would answer, "There's nothing we can do about it, so why get upset?" His apparent unconcern made me feel the more odd and alone. Was I overreacting because I perceived his lack of reaction?

It's crucial to give each other the grace to respond however we need to. As Cheri Fuller and Louise Tucker Jones observe in their book Extraordinary Kids:

> *The way spouses express grief may be poles apart. . . . Men often don't cry or talk about it as readily as their wives, and they may have difficulty reaching out for help. Their tendency is to take action, to try to fix*

things, and they get frustrated when they can't. But when a man is silent, his wife ends up feeling alone and uncomforted in her grief. This pain, if not shared or talked about, can bring increasing distance between the two.[3]

What can we do to bridge the distance in our marriages? Ephesians says we can be kind and compassionate and forgiving with each other (4:32). Together we can carry each other's hurts to the Lord (Gal. 6:2; Eph. 6:18; James 5:16). Truly, He is the one who can heal the brokenhearted (Ps. 147:3).

Turning to the Healer of Our Hearts

Why is the Lord Jesus so able to bind the brokenhearted? Because He Himself was a man well-acquainted with grief, more deeply than we can ever understand, so He is able to comfort us in our grief (see 2 Cor. 1:3—4). When I feel isolated in my sorrow, I've found help in reflecting on Isaiah 53:3—5:

He was despised and rejected by men,
a man of sorrows, and familiar with suffering.
Like one from who men hide their faces
he was despised, and we esteemed him not.
Surely he took up our infirmities
and carried our sorrows,
yet we considered him stricken by God,
smitten by him, and afflicted.
But he was pierced for our transgressions,
he was crushed for our iniquities;
the punishment that brought us peace was upon him,
and by his wounds we are healed.

As deep as our sadness is, Jesus' was worse. To be a timeless, multidimensional being limited to earthly time and space must have felt terribly oppressive. And though He remained unstained by sin, to experience firsthand the struggles we as humans face in temptation and death and everything in between surely caused Him grief. Perhaps it was one thing to know how horrific The Fall was but quite another to actually feel its devastation—it must have been excruciating for our Lord.

I'm not advising anyone to spiritualize grief away; but in reflecting on Christ, I think we're putting into action the counsel of the writer of Hebrews:

> *Let us fix our eyes on Jesus, the author and perfecter of our faith, who for the joy set before him endured the cross, scorning its shame, and sat down at the right hand of the throne of God. Consider him who endured such opposition from sinful men, so that you will not grow weary and lose heart. (Heb. 12:2—3)*

Dear parent, do not grow weary and lose heart. Present your grief and concerns to Christ, who understands what it is to hurt. He will help you endure the mantle of grief until it is lifted permanently on Resurrection Day.

Shock, denial, and grief, of course, are not the only emotions we struggle with. In the next two chapters, we'll look at fear, envy, and anger. These are troublesome feelings, to be sure; but again, God doesn't want any shame over them to keep us from bringing them to Him. Remember what Jesus has revealed about Himself:

> *We do not have a high priest who is unable to sympathize with our weaknesses, but we have one who has been tempted in every way, just as we are. (Heb. 4:15a)*

His feelings didn't lead Him into sin, which ours sometimes do, but this doesn't distance Him from us. Rather, He invites us to come near "the throne of grace with confidence, so that we may receive mercy and find grace to help us in our time of need" (v. 16).

CHAPTER 5

Fear and Faith

I waited patiently for the Lord; he
turned to me and heard my cry.
He lifted me out of the slimy pit,
out of the mud and mire;
he set my feet on a rock and gave
me a firm place to stand.
(Ps. 40:2)

Do you ever feel like your emotions get in the way? I do. I have things to do—I don't have time to cry, be angry, or have a panic attack. My kids need me, and they need me functioning, not trying to stifle tears or rage.

We sometimes feel like our emotions will get the better of us if we allow them to. They will occupy our minds and take over our lives. Sometimes tears are like potato chips—it's hard to stop with just one! Our feelings often color the way we see the world. Anger makes us feel that everything and everyone is out to get us or our child. Grief makes life seem dark and cold, and there's nothing we can do to bring color and warmth to it. Fear makes the world seem dangerous and makes us think that we were born to fail.

If we try to run away from the feelings, they always seem to catch up to us. We hate those feelings and the unsettling things they do to our hearts and minds. Yet, this is how God created us—not as robots, but as human beings who reflect all the things God Himself feels.

How do we reconcile the onslaught of painful emotions with the need to raise our child with a reasonably sane mind?

First, we quit fighting the feelings. If we repress them now, they won't be gone for long. They'll find us. For me personally, I've had to learn not to squelch my feelings, because it hurts my stomach when I do.

Second, we acknowledge them for what they are: just feelings. Even though it may seem like it, emotions won't kill us. They'll make us uncomfortable, for sure, but they aren't deadly.

Third, tell God about it. (Here's a little secret: He already knows.) He is our friend, and He wants to be treated that way. He wants to hear what's on our minds. Also, if we have a trusted earthly friend, one who understands our situation, we should tell that friend. Getting our feelings out in the open and laying them at someone else's feet is often a salve in itself.

Fourth, let God take care of it. I often ask God to take away the feelings because I can't bear the discomfort. But most times, He doesn't. He has a reason for wanting me to ride it out, although I can't understand what it is at the time. If He is our friend, though, we can believe that He will hold our hand. But we have to let Him do that. We'll probably try to pull away and attempt to be brave on our own. He will let us, but we'll wind up hurting ourselves for it.

Last, it helps to know that this will be an ongoing process. Our emotions will recycle perpetually until the day we see Jesus. Let's face it—our children's disabilities aren't going away. The devastating loss of our own dreams and our hopes for a normal life for our kids causes feelings that will never leave us completely. They aren't as intense as in the days of diagnosis, when a fear of the unknown mixed with our grief. We do eventually learn to live a different life, with different stresses than most people, and we can come to accept it as a gift from God. But the reality is that feelings of loss and confusion live within us every day. To be human is to hurt sometimes.

And being human means we'll be scared sometimes, too. Let's get better acquainted with this frequent companion on our journey. We will learn that it's OK to be afraid and that we can move through it. Finally, we'll look at how our faith can help us chart a course through the fearsome storms of our parenting journey.

Fear

Fear is one of the least "acceptable" emotions Christians allow themselves and fellow believers to feel. Most Christians would be surprised to learn how many mothers of children with disabilities are on antidepressants. Fear is particularly often seen as a lack of faith. If we really trusted the Lord to take care of us, we'd face each problem with serenity and strength. Our knees would never knock, our hands would never shake, and our hearts would never pound—if we really believed.

As if a lack of faith weren't enough, some people would like to make us feel that fear is outright disobedience. After all, doesn't Scripture command us again and again to "fear not"? Some preachers will tell us so, but I'm not so sure. I'm not sure this is a command as much as it is a reassurance. Let's look at a couple of passages.

In Matthew 10:28, Jesus tells us, "Do not be afraid of those who kill the body but cannot kill the soul." Now look at the context of this verse. Jesus is reassuring us that the Father has His eyes even on the sparrows and that we are worth much more to Him (vv. 29—31). And He actually encourages us toward a certain kind of fear—the fear of the Lord (v. 28b). His goal is to lead us to the eternal perspective, and His tone is loving, not berating.

In another situation, Jesus told His disciples on the night He was to be crucified, "Do not let your hearts be troubled and do not be afraid" (John 14:27). Was this a commandment with an "or else" attached to it? No, the context is one of comfort, encouragement, and preparation for the horror the disciples would soon face.

Please don't get me wrong—I'm not trying to encourage you to let fear take over your life. But I want to relieve you of any false guilt you may have for feeling fearful about your child's future and your ability to handle it. In our situation, fear is not necessarily a lack of faith or disobedience; we have real reasons for being fearful.

Sometimes, though, we don't know exactly why we're afraid. Part of our task, then, is to find out what's causing our fear. Only then do we have hope in releasing fear's stranglehold.

When We Don't Know Why We're Afraid

When our fear is vague and free-floating, it often sneaks up and ambushes us. If you've ever experienced a panic attack, you know what I mean. A panic attack is like having a hood thrown over your head and a noose tightened around your neck.

The first time I had a panic attack, I was minding my own business, eating a meal in a restaurant. All of a sudden my heart began to race and my vision dimmed. I turned cold and clammy and seemed to lose my ability to breathe. This feeling came from nowhere. I remember wondering if I was having I having a bad reaction to some new medication. Am I having a heart attack? What in the world is happening to me? A trip to the urgent care facility revealed nothing. Nothing was happening to me at all, the doctor said. I was just a little high-strung, and he told me to go home and take it easy.

Go home and take it easy—with two kids with special needs? Now that was a trick! I had specialists to go to, paperwork to fill out, and programs to monitor. I didn't have any chances to take it easy. I did my best to relax, but that smothering feeling kept happening. It seemed to reach down without warning and scoop my insides out. It happened at home, at the store, in the morning, at noon, and during the night. In fact, it happened mostly at night, preventing me from falling asleep or staying asleep. I was miserable.

What I didn't know then was that in panic attacks, the sufferer has a false sense of smothering because he or she is hyperventilating. The hyperventilation causes a reduction of blood flow to the brain, which is interpreted as a sign of suffocation. Just what we need when coping with stress—less blood to the brain!

Panic attacks can be free-floating; that is, they can come at any moment and last for any length of time. We can be driven to desperation when we don't know why we're having these attacks and to not know how to get rid of them. We can feel claustrophobic in our own bodies. And it seems that the harder we try to control them, the worse they get. Several times I found myself with numb hands and arms, and even legs. Now that's some serious hyperventilating!

We often think, if we can only figure out what is causing this fear, maybe we can eliminate the panic attacks. We can become almost more afraid of the feeling of fear than the reason behind it. Yet, as hard as we try to search through the murkiness of our thoughts and feelings, we can't quite seem to put our finger on it. What are we really afraid of?

Why Are We Afraid?

Our fears stem from a variety of reasons. Let's look at several that I've found are quite common among the families I have talked with.

1. Loss of Control

Behind the fear that many parents deal with is the feeling of powerlessness. Having a child with special needs shatters one of our most trusted illusions: that we are in control. Our child's disabilities shine a stark, merciless light on the reality of what little control we actually have over our world. We may not have consciously thought we were in control; as Christians, we're taught that God, in His sovereignty, superintends everything. Yet we may have thought subconsciously that we were pulling some strings. A prayer here, an act of kindness there, plus faithful worship should equal earthly reward, right?

We may be reluctant to confess that we've thought that way, but our reaction to our child's needs belies our thinking. When our child requires extra help, we feel that we've made a mistake somehow. We've goofed up the formula. And suddenly we realize that maybe there is no formula. Maybe we can't guarantee our safety through right decisions and actions. And the reality of our vulnerability shakes us to our core.

We've already seen that even when we make every right decision——we've taken our prenatal vitamins, we've eaten well, we've avoided medications during pregnancy, we've sought good, regular medical attention——we can still give birth to a child with special needs. We attempt to control our own circumstances. We don't realize that when we get the outcome we had hoped for, it isn't because we've manipulated events or

God. It's because God has bestowed blessings on us—just as He wants to.

Realizing that we really never had the ability to control our lives can be frightening. But remember, the hand that controls everything is the same hand that grabs ours when we start to feel ourselves falling. Focusing on this can help take some of the fear away.

Wanting to be in control is a desire that's been with us all our lives, so how do we let go of this cherished illusion? We need to make a daily abdication to the One who sits on the throne of heaven. In the prayer that Jesus taught His disciples, He began with a focus on God's nature and His will:

> "'Our Father in heaven,
> hallowed be your name,
> your kingdom come,
> your will be done
> on earth as it is in heaven.'"
> (Matt. 6:9—10, emphasis added)

This should be part of our every prayer, because releasing control of our lives is not natural to us. Submitting to God requires a relinquishing, not only of one's actions, but of one's heart. And a heart isn't an easy thing to give up. That's why God asks us to do only what we can: give our heart and our will up to Him one day at a time.

I have to admit that doing this is very difficult for me. I like the "prepayment submission plan" idea: I agree to submit to God's will, He accepts me at my word, and I never again struggle with the notion that His control is superior to mine. Unfortunately, it doesn't work that way. Being a person who worries about how things are going to work out, I have a multitude of backup plans. But what backup plan can we have when our children have special needs? There isn't one, and God doesn't need us to develop one. His original plan is sufficient. God's ideas and ways are superior to ours. And we can give Him our fear as we bow to that.

2. *The Situation Is Beyond Our Capabilities*

Another cause for our fear is the worry that our children's situation is beyond our capabilities. And it is. How in the world are we supposed to know how to make good decisions about our child's care? We have no experience at this. As new parents, we still have to learn about all the ordinary stuff—feeding and diapering, comforting and teaching. But now we have to make choices above and beyond those things. We need to choose an appropriate program, the right doctors and teachers, the most beneficial health care and behavioral interventions.

And it doesn't help that we've been taught to take care of ourselves. Our culture, both secular and religious, trumpets those who are strong, who make right decisions, and who are blessed because of it. We don't want to make mistakes, and if we do, we certainly don't want anyone to know about them. So, now that we are charged with taking care of children who need us to make right decisions for them, what if we make the wrong choice? That possibility scares us to death.

The one thing we do know for sure is that raising our child alone—without God's help—is impossible. We are acutely aware that we are fallible and that our decisions will affect our child's long-term future. What if we make our child worse? What if we blow the one opportunity to "save" our children from the effects of their disability? Every decision becomes fraught with fear: What if . . .

We have to learn to give our burdens and decision-making to God. That in itself is scary, because maybe we're not sure if we're hearing His voice correctly. All we can do is pray about it, lay it down, and know that, even if it appears that we've made a grave mistake, God will bring good out of it. We've got to let it go. God often doesn't expect as much of us as we do of ourselves. So give it up. It is beyond your capability—but it isn't beyond God's. (We'll look at this more in-depth in chapter 7.)

3. *Exposing Our Doubts*

A third cause for fear is letting others see our doubts and weaknesses. How many of us have been told, "God chose you for a reason"—and had that person smile confidently at us? But

I don't know why God chose me. Do you know why God chose you? I wouldn't have picked me! Someone with my personality and fears doesn't seem to me to be the best candidate. Do these smiling people know something we don't?

No, but for some reason, we hate to let them down. We want to live up to their faith in us. We often can't, however, and we wind up feeling like weak people masquerading as strong ones.

If we come clean as the confused people we are, are we letting our encouragers down? Do we shake their faith in God if we tell them we're terrified? When they tell us, "God never gives you more than you can bear," is our witness as Christ's ambassadors damaged if we voice our doubts about His sovereign will?

Some of this fear is based on pride. We don't want to look weak. We don't want to be branded as doubters. We don't want to be poor witnesses for Christ. Won't people be disappointed in us if they know what we're really thinking? Will they reject us as heretics? There's a lot at stake in being honest with others. We run the risk of having them misunderstand and walk away.

But you know what? The only antidote I've found for pride, or for fearing looking bad to others, is confession. Not just confession to God in secret, but coming clean with another person. Giving voice to our doubts makes us vulnerable, which is why we need to choose our confessors carefully. It's usually wise to seek out someone who has also walked a difficult road. Do you know someone who has suffered a great loss—and has been burnished by the experience rather than beaten down? Do you know someone with the gift of listening? Ask this person out for coffee or drop them a note with your question. This can be not only a time of relief for you but also a chance for him or her to use their gift of compassion.

If you can't think of anyone to share your concerns with, pray that God will lead you to the person you need. It may take time, but God will be faithful in providing just the right one. His choice may surprise you; it may be someone you know well or someone you just met. In the meantime, keep talking honestly with the Lord about your struggles. This may be difficult—it may feel irreverent or distrustful. But He already knows what is going on inside your head and heart, so taking your doubts to Him is actually a show of trust.

4. God Has Left Us

Probably one of our greatest fears is that somehow God has abandoned us. We may feel that God has let us down, and we're afraid He'll do it again. This makes us fear the future, because we're not sure God is there.

I don't know why I can't seem to remember the times God has upheld me when I'm going through a painful time. Or maybe I do remember, but for some reason I fear that He will get tired of helping me. Do you sometimes feel this way too? This thinking actually brings God down to a human level—we fear burning him out. But God can't get burned out. As Scripture tells us (and something we need to remind ourselves of often):

Why do you say, O Jacob,
and complain, O Israel,
"My way is hidden from the LORD;
my cause is disregarded by my God"?
Do you not know?
Have you not heard?
The LORD is the everlasting God,
the Creator of the ends of the earth.
He will not grow tired or weary,
and his understanding no one can fathom.
(Isa. 40:27—28)

And the psalmist reassures us that the Lord "knows how we are formed, he remembers that we are dust" (Ps. 103:14).

Even though we know in our heads that God is with us, it doesn't always feel like it, does it? In our deepest grief, we can feel His presence slipping away. It terrifies us to think that we grieve alone, that we will have to walk alone, that the one person we need most has gone away. We know it really isn't happening, but we feel it anyway. The psalmists felt it, the great Christian writer C. S. Lewis felt it, and St. John of the Cross even had a name for it—the "dark night of the soul." People always reassure us that God hasn't gone anywhere during our trials. But we feel completely alone.

What is at the root of this? Perhaps it's expecting something more from God than we feel we're getting. When my husband and I discovered that our younger son, then an infant, would need neurosurgery, I felt a sadness I had not felt before. I was also afraid of what this surgery might mean for our future. As I made my need known to God and to our fellowship group at church, I felt a peace that went beyond all human comprehension. I knew that God would take care of our son, whether in life or in death, and I knew He would take care of us. I marveled as the Scriptures about God's care became real to me.

So years later, after all the assurances that our son would be fine, the news that he had a disability was a real shock. I expected God to comfort me in exactly the same way He had before. I expected that, even in my sadness, I would feel peace. But I didn't. When I reached out to grab the comforting hand, I felt air instead. What was wrong?

I came to realize that when everything I thought I was had been stripped away; at the core of me was nothing but fear. As long as I kept focusing on that, I couldn't see anything else. My feelings were screaming so loud that they drowned out God's voice.

I do believe that rampant fear is one of Satan's best weapons. If we stay mired in panic, we have a hard time moving toward God's grace. If Satan can convince us that God really doesn't care—or that He doesn't even exist—then half the battle is lost. Feeling fear is not an indication of a lack of faith, but becoming a slave to fear is not what God has intended. This fear of God leaving us is best fought with the shield of faith (see Eph. 6:16).

The Shielding Role of Faith

Faith starts to allay our fears when we act on our knowledge rather than on our emotion. Philip Yancey, in his book <u>Disappointment with God</u>, writes:

> We may experience times of unusual closeness, when every prayer is answered in an obvious way and God seems intimate and caring. And we may also

experience "fog times," when God stays silent, when nothing works according to formula and all the Bible's promises seem glaringly false. Fidelity involves learning to trust that, out beyond the perimeter of fog, God still reigns and has not abandoned us, no matter how it may appear.[1]

This is what it boils down to: we can still feel the fear, but we have to choose to supersede it with small acts of obedience. Attending worship, reading the Scriptures, singing praise songs—-even though none of it may make any sense to us, we need to do them anyway. They may not feel natural; they didn't to me. Half the time I felt like a fraud sitting in the church pews, and I hoped no one would find out. Maybe that's why I had some of my worst panic attacks in church. And maybe that's why so many people I've talked with have their panic attacks in church also.

Also, acting on faith doesn't necessarily mean feeling that faith. Have you ever thought that people of great faith never doubted, that it was always easy for them to believe? In reality, it isn't that way at all. We may believe God's promises in our heads, but when we face our child's disability, it's a struggle to believe them in our hearts. This is where the work of faith comes in. It takes conscious effort to root out our fears and replace them with the abiding peace of God. This won't come instantly; it's a process. But it's something we need to apply ourselves to. We need to work at believing the Lord when He says,

"For I am the LORD, your God,
who takes hold of your right hand
and says to you, Do not fear;
I will help you." (Isa. 41:13)

CHAPTER 6

The Dark Side: Envy and Anger

*Who is wise and understanding among you? Let
him show it by his good life, by deeds done in the
humility that comes from wisdom. But if you harbor
bitter envy and selfish ambition in your hearts, do
not boast about it or deny the truth.*

*"In your anger do not sin": Do not let the sun go
down while you are still angry, and do not give the
devil a foothold.*
(JAMES 3:13—14; EPH. 4:26—27)

The emotions of envy and anger are especially difficult for us
to accept and handle because the Bible admonishes us to not
let either of these gain a foothold in our lives (see 2 Cor. 12:20;
Gal. 5:20). To allow these emotions to consume and control us is
to allow Satan to enter (Eph. 4:26—27). And to be honest, unlike
grief and fear, envy and anger can make us scary people. An
envious person can make us feel bad about the blessings God
has given us. And being with an angry person is like being on
continual red alert—the danger of an imminent explosion keeps
our nerves taut and our minds tense. If we nurse these emotions
they will mutate into bitterness, which poisons everything it
touches.

Let's take a closer look at these troublesome emotions for
parents of children with special needs.

Envy

Envy usually surfaces when we look at others who have seemingly perfect homes, children, and lives; and we wonder why we didn't get some of that—even just a little.

They have quiet, smart, well-behaved children who walk, talk, and sleep through the night, who don't wear diapers or need a wheelchair, and who win awards and excel at sports. They can take wonderful, lavish family vacations, getting lots of enjoyment and rest; while our children may not even be able to sit in a car, and the daily grind of their care wears us down. They have lovely homes, nice furniture, and beautiful clothes; while our money goes to doctors, medications, and special equipment.

It's so easy to covet the apparent tranquility they have, the admiration their children receive, and the opportunities they have to share their triumphs with others.

These envious reveries, though, usually result in guilt— because we do love our children deeply, and we don't want someone else's family. We don't want to devalue our children by thinking we'd be happier if they could accomplish more. And we don't want to challenge God's wisdom and goodness to us.

How can we avoid the trap of envy? I think Jesus, Peter, and John each give us an important clue. In the last chapter of the Gospel of John, Jesus gave Peter a glimpse into his future:

> *"I tell you the truth, when you were younger you*
> *dressed yourself and went where you wanted; but*
> *when you are old you will stretch out your hands, and*
> *someone else will dress you and lead you where you do*
> *not want to go." Jesus said this to indicate the kind of*
> *death by which Peter would glorify God. (John 21:18—*
> *19a)*

Jesus' next words to Peter centered on a command to keep his eyes on Christ: "Follow me!" (v. 19b). But Peter, still the impetuous soul, turned around and looked at John and asked Jesus what would happen to him. Was Peter simply curious? Was he uncomfortable with what his future held when he enviously wondered if John, the disciple whom Jesus loved, would get something better? And if John did get something less painful than Peter, did this mean that Jesus loved John more than Peter?

Can you identify with Peter? I can. Because I sometimes I feel the same way. Does Jesus love parents of typical children more than He does parents of kids with special needs? Do you ever secretly wonder about that? For me, that insidious, menacing question may be the root of my envy.

But look at how Jesus answered Peter: "If I want him to remain alive until I return, what is that to you? You must follow me" (v. 22). Our Lord gives no lengthy explanation and no balm for a bruised ego; He simply reminds Peter to stop looking at his neighbor and follow the Leader. In essence, Jesus says, "Don't look at anybody else. You look at Me. I am the only One who matters."

Fixing our eyes on Jesus—and keeping them there—will keep us from looking over the fence and envying someone else's "greener" grass. Truth be told, the grass is rarely greener on the other side—sometimes we're just seeing Astroturf! Real grass, in contrast, has weeds and bugs and the occasional dry patch. God has given us our lawn, and we need to follow the Master Gardener in order to maintain and enjoy it. When we're busy consulting Him, we won't have time to climb the fence and peek over at our neighbors. Remember Jesus' words: "What is that to you? You must follow Me."

Anger

Sometimes, in our unique situations, we can't help feeling angry—and often our reasons are legitimate. When a doctor or specialist ignores our concerns about our children, we feel angry. When educators don't follow our children's special education plan, we feel angry. When our children's peers make fun of them for being different, we feel angry. And when our peers and family members can't understand and when our family is stared at, ignored, or condescended to by others, we feel very angry. Anger is a valid and realistic feeling in these situations because people are being insensitive, careless, or just plain mean.

Being angry with unperceptive people is one thing, but what about being angry with God? Is it acceptable to be mad at Him, or are we committing a sin? And anyway, why would we be angry at the Lord who loves us? I can share lots of reasons that perhaps sound familiar to you—because you may have them yourself.

Part of what was fueling my panic attacks was unrecognized anger directed at God. When I finally discovered that anger was behind some of my fear, I also uncovered an irate dialogue (or monologue) directed at God that my heart had valiantly tried to conceal: How could You do this to me? Wasn't I pleasing You enough? What do You want from me anyway? This isn't fair! Do You call this "love"? Like a child who screams at her parents for not getting what she wants, I wanted to yell at God, "I don't like You right now! You're making me mad!"

This is scary ground to tread on. It's no light thing for sinners to be angry with the living God. As Moses wrote:

Who knows the power of your anger?
For your wrath is as great as the fear that is due you.
(Ps. 90:11)

And like Job's counselor Elihu, we ask,

Do you think I'm dumb enough to challenge God?
Wouldn't that just be asking for trouble?
No one in his right mind stares straight at the sun
on a clear and cloudless day.
As gold comes from the northern mountains,
so a terrible beauty streams from God. (Job 37:20—22
THE MESSAGE)[1]

If God has already allowed disability to enter our lives, what worse thing is He holding back? If God is already mad at us, we sure don't want to upset Him further by complaining!

However, as in all close relationships, if we are angry—even if we don't realize it ourselves—the other person can often sense that something's amiss. So, doesn't God, who knows the number of hairs on our heads (Matt. 10:30), already know that we're angry? He knows our hearts better than we do; He isn't fooled by our emotional camouflage. And if we want a close relationship with Him, we need to get our feelings out in the open; we can't give God the silent treatment. And we can't pretend we don't feel the way we do.

We need to take David's insight into God to heart: "Behold, You desire truth in the innermost being, And in the hidden part You will make me know wisdom" (Ps. 51:6 NASB). So what does God say about being angry in His Word?

First, it is acceptable to be angry; we just can't become angry people. Ephesians 4:26—27 puts it this way: "Go ahead and be angry. You do well to be angry—but don't use your anger as fuel for revenge. And don't stay angry. Don't go to bed angry. Don't give the Devil that kind of foothold in your life" (THE MESSAGE).[2]

Dealing with our anger is often a process that takes time. We may not be able to resolve it completely before bedtime— however, we should at least be moving toward resolving it by then. Anger is not something we want to hold onto. Rather, we need to start the process of working through it, because only then will we find healing and a renewed relationship.

When anger becomes our focus and stops us from doing what we need to do, we may need help. Satan will do all he can to keep us angry and separated from God. Ruth, whose son Christopher has autism, describes her struggle with anger and what felt like Satan's oppression:

> *There was just so much we were going through. And I needed to deal with the anger, and I did. . . .*
> *It was hard to be close and feel close to God. Going to church was extremely difficult. I felt like a hypocrite. I didn't want to sing the songs. I didn't get joy out of the music like I usually do. I was there because that's where I had to be. And some of the things the minister was saying I knew I needed to hear.*
> *And Satan was really battling. It felt like he was ever-present and that he was trying to get his way with me. It was very, very hard.*
> *I didn't feel like worshiping in my heart. I knew in my head that it was the right thing to go to church, but I think I was closing myself up and not allowing myself to feel God's presence because I felt Satan had a hold on*

me. . . And I didn't feel that I knew how to control that. And that's why I went through some lay counseling, to give me some tools to fight the oppression.

Ruth was wise to seek counseling. Unfortunately, too many of us view asking for help as a sign of weakness or failure because we're supposed to be "mature" Christians. Sometimes this stems from pride; sometimes it comes from fear of being a less than stellar spiritual model for others. But pride and fear can keep us from the truth, and the truth is where God wants us to be. So if we have a need, we should face it and seek out trusted and discreet Christian help from a pastor, a mentor, or a professional counselor.

At the start of this discussion on anger I asked the question, Is it acceptable to be mad at God, or are we committing a sin? I think we are allowed to challenge God occasionally, even though it may not be our right.

Do you remember the story of Jacob wrestling with God? Jacob had spent the day in some anxiety as he prepared to meet his brother Esau for the first time since he stole his birthright. After he had sent his family across the stream Jabbok, he alone remained in the camp—except for an anonymous visitor:

So Jacob was left alone, and a man wrestled with him till daybreak. When the man saw that he could not overpower him, he touched the socket of Jacob's hip so that his hip was wrenched as he wrestled with the man. Then the man said, "Let me go, for it is daybreak."

But Jacob replied, "I will not let you go unless you bless me."

The man asked him, "What is your name?"

"Jacob," he answered.

Then the man said, "Your name will no longer be Jacob, but Israel, because you have struggled with God and with men and have overcome."

Jacob said, "Please tell me your name."

But he replied, "Why do you ask my name?" Then he blessed him there.

So Jacob called the place Peniel, saying, "It is

because I saw God face to face and yet my life was spared." (Gen. 32:24—30)

God, in the form of an angel, allowed Jacob to wrestle with Him. "Jacob had struggled all his life to prevail, first with Esau, then with Laban. Now, as he was about to reenter Canaan, he was shown that it was with God that he must 'wrestle.'"[3] In the form He took, God showed that Jacob was allowed to wrestle with Him—but the Lord still had the power to disable Jacob with just one touch. He could have taken Jacob's life, but He didn't. Instead, He gave Jacob a permanent limp, which was a visible reminder of the power of the living God to wound and to heal.

We, too, may need to wrestle with God; begging for an answer; begging for release; begging, like Jacob, for a blessing. In our wrestling, we may not want to worship the Lord; we may be too angry at Him or we may not be sure He's even there. But He knows what we need, and He can handle it. He will preserve our life, but He may leave us with some form of limp as a reminder of our encounter with Him. It's comforting to remember that "the Lord is compassionate and gracious, slow to anger, abounding in love" (Ps. 103:8). His compassion and grace can diffuse our anger—but only if we bring it to Him and allow Him to heal in His way.

Trusting through All of Our Emotions

We've thought a lot about our feelings in the past three chapters, and now we need to look in more detail at the role of our faith. Are we in an either/or situation: either we trust God or revel in our feelings? Are faith and feelings mutually exclusive? As you can probably gather by now, my answer is, "Absolutely not!" Our faith and our feelings have to go hand in hand in a balanced way.

I haven't come to this conclusion easily. I would rather not have to deal with the ups and downs of my feelings all the time. I tend to get caught up in the myth that in order to function properly, I must abandon my troublesome feelings. In order to be effective in my children's lives, I need to be in top form emotionally—feeling no pain. I sometimes think that if I really trusted God, I wouldn't feel anxious, sad, angry, confused, or anything else.

But I also know that denying what I feel is not living in truth. Life is not pure reason and logic, and neither is faith.

So, what should you do when your feelings seem to overwhelm you or begin to interfere with your daily activities? For starters, try not to spend valuable time and energy on attempting to escape your emotions. For example, don't ask God to take the feelings away. That's tempting to do, but it usually results in disappointment when He doesn't. Instead, focus on the fact that God has it all under control already—and He loves us immensely. Learn to work at trusting Him to take care of you and your child.

And yes, that's work. As Jesus said in John 6:29, "The work of God is this: to believe in the one he has sent." Believing that God is who He says He is and that He will do what He has said He will do is not easy when our feelings tell us just the opposite. We need to feel our feelings, but we still need to believe the Lord.

One thing I've noticed as I've grown older is that my body has developed aches and pains that don't like to go away. If I waited for nothing in my body to hurt before I did anything, I'd be in bed all day long. So I just keep going. On bad days, I may need some ibuprofen, but I still keep going.

The same is true emotionally. Our feelings don't define our life; our faith does. Our feelings are not our life's rudder; our faith is. So no matter what we're feeling, we still need to obey God—-keep going in the task He has called us to. Our feelings matter to God, certainly; but I think our obedience to Him matters more. When He says, "Trust me," I don't have to feel it—I have to do it. Trust is more muscular than we usually think.

I don't consider myself to be a person of great faith. Those who know me understand that I almost always look at the glass half empty. And God knows it too. So when I choose to trust Him, it is an act of the will, not always of the heart. For example, when I ask Him for help, I have to decide that He is going to help me—that He wants to help me. That's trust. It doesn't mean that I don't have doubts or feel bad, but I choose by an act of obedience to believe in my mind that God knows what He's doing with me and with my child. Part of me will always wonder what God has in mind, but that's for Him to work out, not me. When I focus on God and His infinite ways, I find that the pain of my uncomfortable feelings diminishes.

Scripture tells us that what we face here on earth is not all there is. We may seem locked into this temporal setting, but eternity is nearer than we think. In this light, we can put our emotions into perspective. What eternal significance will our feelings have? I don't know. But I do know that our acts of obedience will stand forever (see 1 Cor. 3:10—15).

All of us are created differently; some of us feel things intensely, while others barely feel anything at all. God created us this way on purpose. We glorify Him in

- loving Him, despite our tears,
- trusting Him, despite our fears,
- thanking Him, despite our wants, and
- submitting to Him, despite our anger.

When we choose to believe that God sees all of our hurts, cares about us immensely, and has a purpose behind our struggles, we place more bricks into our foundation of faith. And our faith is more precious than gold (1 Peter 1:7). Here's something to trust in:

"For the Lamb at the center of the throne will be their shepherd;
he will lead them to springs of living water.
And God will wipe away every tear from their eyes."
(Rev. 7:17; see also 21:1—5)

The Unexpected Gift

Chapter 7

Perfected in Weakness

*But he said to me, "My grace is sufficient for you,
for my power is made perfect in weakness."*
(2 Cor. 12:9)

"God never gives us more than we can handle."
Oh, really?
I'm not sure I agree with this bit of "comfort" anymore. How about you? I know for a fact that I can't handle all that has been handed to me with my own strength. And from seeing others falter under their load—conscientious Christians who have nervous breakdowns, for example—I know that this saying cannot be true. Yet this rosy-colored idea still persists and is actively promoted.

Certain Christian radio and TV programs and books contend that if we can't master a problem, we (1) are not strong enough, (2) don't have enough faith, or (3) are doing something wrong. But ask any recovering alcoholic or drug addict, or ask anyone who struggles with chronic illness, and they'll tell you that certain things in life are definitely beyond our own ability to conquer.

As parents of children with special needs, we know the feeling of wanting our children to be healed, both for their sakes and for ours. We know what it is to be powerless to change our child's situation. And we know the limitations imposed on our families because of disability. We're faced daily with the truth that much of life is beyond our capacity to control or change.

So maybe we need to make a slight change in the wording of that saying: "God never gives us more than He can handle."

In this chapter, I want to focus on what it means to let God perfect His power in our weakness, to let His grace be sufficient for us. Because if there's anybody in need of God's power and grace in his or her life—it's the parent of a child with special needs.

Our Weakness

In our American culture, because it's drummed into our heads that we must be independent and strong, coming to terms with our weakness is no easy matter. From toddler-hood, we declare, "I'll do it myself!" We enjoy being strong. We like it when people compliment our strength. We want to be seen as brave, clever, and completely able to manage on our own.

This kind of thinking seeps into our unique calling as parents of children with disabilities. We can do one of two things: First, we can decide that it's all up to us to "fix" our child. We want to secure the best treatment, the finest doctors, the most effective therapies—anything to help our child. With each disability, we search for a "miracle cure" that usually involves lots of money, excessive time, or both. While some people are helped by these therapies, many heartbroken families aren't, even though they've sacrificed everything. They often end up believing that somehow they have failed. They didn't administer the medications correctly or do the exercises properly. It wasn't the therapy that failed; something they did wrong caused the therapy to fail. Their sense of "failure" too often spirals into a pit of judgment and guilt.

On the other hand, we parents of special children can take on a false bravado, where our heads are held high and our tears are under control. Underneath this veneer, we may be a quivering mass of insecure jelly, but how we love to be praised for our superior handling of our special task. We may even deliberately perpetuate the myth that we're made of Teflon so that others can see why God chose us to parent this special child. Yes, we were specially selected for this task because we are somehow inherently stronger and braver than the rest of the population. Those with typical children must be weaker people, unable to stand the rigors of our assignment!

This thinking usually works for about five minutes.

Our weakness soon shatters our pride when our child is hospitalized, goes through a regressive period, or stays up all night for weeks at a time. We may ask our bodies to do inhuman things—skip meals to keep up with busy schedules, miss sleep to stay up with restless children, forgo our own doctor's appointments to accommodate everyone else's needs—but we'll find that our bodies can't keep pace for long.

Our minds will let us down too. We may try hard to not be disappointed when therapies don't work, or attempt to not get too attached to our child when he or she doesn't know us, but we eventually come crashing down.

Sometimes we can't imagine how we'll make it through another day without cracking up. Things just get to be too much. Physically, emotionally, spiritually—in every area all our resources are drained. We may need to be under a doctor's care. We may need medications like antidepressants or tranquilizers. We may need to ask friends to help with everyday household tasks. How humbling. Our façade of strength is revealed, and our weakness is fully exposed.

As Barb, who son Brad has multiple special needs, observes, "When there are outside issues, like work problems or other stresses, my coping skills aren't always as good. I find more grieving occurring when I am also dealing with stresses that are unrelated to my son's disabilities." Even small stresses can sometimes tip us into overload. Take the disgruntled customer on the other side of the counter, for example, who doesn't know that you've been up half the night with a child who refuses to sleep. Or the lady who cuts in line at the supermarket, who doesn't care that you've got just three seconds before your child with autism throws a tantrum. (She will care, though, and she'll probably give you dirty looks for it.)

Few people outside our homes know the daily pressures we face in parenting children with special needs. The stress doesn't come just from these responsibilities—it comes from the addition of all the ordinary responsibilities that don't go away. We still have jobs to go to, bills to pay, relatives to take care of, funerals to attend, marriages to work on, and other children to nurture.

We have no visible marker, like the black armbands of mourning from years ago, to let people know what we're going through. If our child does not have obvious physical or mental disabilities, or if we're not with our child at the time, there is nothing to tell others that we may be in a fragile emotional state or exhausted. There's no sign telling others, "Tread lightly, be kind, I'm tired."

In truth, we aren't special or chosen; only our circumstances are. We are fragile, we are needy, and we are weak. But God is strong, and He is on our side.

God's Strength

In 2 Corinthians 12, Paul exposes his own weakness. We don't usually think of Paul as weak, but he was painfully human like the rest of us. Here is how Eugene Peterson renders Paul's words:

> *I don't want anyone imagining me as anything other than the fool you'd encounter if you saw me on the street or heard me talk.*
>
> *Because of the extravagance of [the revelations God gave me], and so I wouldn't get a big head, I was given the gift of a handicap to keep me in constant touch with my limitations. Satan's angel did his best to get me down; what he in fact did was push me to my knees. No danger then of walking around high and mighty! At first I didn't think of it as a gift, and begged God to remove it. Three times I did that, and then he told me,*
>
> *"My grace is enough; it's all you need.*
> *My strength comes into its own in your weakness."*
>
> *Once I heard that, I was glad to let it happen. I quit focusing on the handicap and began appreciating the gift. It was a case of Christ's strength moving in on my weakness. Now I take limitations in stride, and with good cheer, these limitations that cut me down to size—abuse, accidents, opposition, bad breaks. I just let Christ take over! And so the weaker I get, the stronger I become. (2 Cor. 12:6—10 THE MESSAGE)[1]*

How do we come to this place that Paul did? How do we let Christ's strength move in on our weakness?

Realize, above all else, that it won't happen overnight. Learning how to rely on God for our strength is an ongoing, lifelong process. I used to believe that each difficult experience would bring me more and more strength so that toward the end of my Christian walk I would be a woman of steel. But then I realized that if this were true, I wouldn't have much need for Christ. I will always need Christ. We all need Him and always will.

We tend to beat ourselves up when we have weak moments, moments when we seem to have forgotten everything we ever learned about Christ and His sufficient grace. Shouldn't we be stronger now? Shouldn't we be less upset about things that cause us grief, whether they are related to disability or not? Maybe not. But we should be more mature in the knowledge that, despite our feeling weak and inadequate, God is always tough enough to fight our battles for us.

What this requires, though, is acknowledging our own weaknesses and limitations. This is something I don't like to do, and you probably don't either. From childhood and throughout our lives, we hide our weaknesses. We stuff messes under the bed; we pretend we really didn't trip on that crack in the sidewalk; we bite the inside of our cheek and fight back those tears with everything we've got. The idea is to appear much smarter, stronger, happier, and surer of ourselves than we really are in the mistaken belief that people (and maybe even God) will like us better this way.

I personally hate admitting that I can't do something. I get so mad at myself for not being able to figure out how to get total control over my sons' disabilities that I lose sight of the fact that I don't have to master them. God knows I have no idea what I'm doing, and it's OK with Him. I need to remember that we all have limitations and weaknesses—that's being human; we're wired that way. If we were perfect, we would be Christ, and we wouldn't need Him.

It takes time and practice to understand how to face and accept our weaknesses and turn them over to God. I laugh at myself because when I first wrote this chapter, I seemed to have a grip on what it takes to always rely on God's perfect grace. As

I refine these words, though, I find that I have to go back and see just what I wrote. What were those little nuggets of wisdom I had discovered? As I go through dark days again, I seem to have forgotten them all. Why doesn't the knowledge seem to stick?

Accepting our weaknesses and handing them to God is a daily and sometimes hourly task. Just as we don't give a yearly prayer and expect it to "cover" all of our needs, desires, and transgressions, so we can't expect to declare our failings and have God put an annual salve on our wounds. We will never reach a state on this earth where our weakness—whether emotional or physical—will be eliminated. It is much like our children's disabilities—they will never be free of them this side of eternity.

Paul was never free of his thorn in the flesh, remember? As commentator Paul Barnett notes:

> In practical terms it means that we accept that we live in God's "plan B" world and that the "plan A" world is yet to come. In this present world there are injustice and inequality, and frequently we are helpless to remedy the evil effects of these in our own lives. In this present existence we suffer from disorders within our personalities, and though prayer and counseling may minimize them but they are not always removed. In our present lives many suffer from ill-health, mental illness and disease that neither intercession nor medication overcomes. What is the Christian to do in these circumstances of pain and suffering? He is to pray that the Lord will deliver him, as Paul did. It may be that God will deliver the person, as he is continuously doing (2 Cor. 1:10; 4:7—10), mindful that all such deliverances are partial. But if not, what then? It is all too easy to allow these things to eat away at our lives until we become embittered and self-pitying. . . . The person in Christ is to allow those "thorns" to pin him closer to Christ who imparts grace to the sufferer both to bear the pain and also to develop qualities of endurance and patience.
>
> In some mysterious way it is within God's plan that our present existence is marked by sin and suffering.

*From one point of view God abhors and hates these
things and will one day overthrow them. And yet is it
not through the awareness of our sins that the grace of
God holds us near Christ for forgiveness right through
our lives? And is it not, also, in the pain of the suffering
of both body and mind, that the same grace pins us
closer to Christ, who says to us, "My power is made
perfect in weakness"?* [2]

If we could rid ourselves of everything that drags us down—
bouts with depression, our feelings of inadequacy, our children's
disabilities—what would we do then? When Paul prayed to be
released from his thorn, why did God leave it in?

He did it in order to demonstrate Christ's power through
Paul's weakness. Paul reasons that the thorn kept him humble.
So do our thorns (I confess, though, I resent them terribly at
times). We may wish things were perfect instead of a mess. We
may wish we were strong instead of weak. But that's not the
world we live in.

Interestingly, our world is imperfect even from a scientific
standpoint. An article in <u>The Los Angeles Times</u> states the
physicists' view of our imperfect world:

*The closer physicists get to understanding the
fundamental laws that rule the universe, the closer to
perfect symmetry they come. And yet, our universe is
far from this perfect state of grace: Forces are different
from particles; electrons are different from quarks;
gravity is different from electricity; and matter is
different from antimatter.*

*"The reality we observe in our laboratories is only an
imperfect reflection of a deeper, more beautiful
reality," writes physicist Steven Weinberg. Physicists like
Weinberg are in search of an ultimate theory of physics
that displays "all the symmetries" of this lost perfection.* [3]

The article goes on to hypothesize why the universe is
composed of "broken symmetries". After reading the author's
explanation, I admit I still don't quite understand the atomic
formula that causes the brokenness. I do know that at one time,

as the Scriptures state, our world was perfect; but through our own rebellion, flaws entered into the perfection.

Christ came to atone for our rebellions, our sins, our imperfections. All we need to do is accept that and allow Him to begin perfecting us—making us more whole. When we become exhausted or flummoxed by our situation, we can rely on the One who is perfect symmetry. As the prophet Isaiah encouraged us:

> *He gives strength to the weary*
> *and increases the power of the weak. (Isa. 40:29)*

Only by allowing ourselves to recognize our deep poverty of strength and sufficiency can we begin to experience God's grace and strength. Remember,

> *"Blessed are the poor in spirit . . . blessed are those*
> *who mourn . . . blessed are the meek" (Matt. 5:3—5).*

Now, God's strength may not come as we expect it. We probably won't have perfect rest and peace and superhuman energy. But we will have the ability to perform those things that God would have us do. Through Him, we will be able to meet the needs, and sometimes the desires, of our children and spouse. Through Him, we will be able to make it through all the meetings we don't want to go to and all the phone calls we don't want to make. We may not be dancing on air, but we'll get what needs doing done.

And we'll know He has helped us because in retrospect, we will ask ourselves how in the world we made it over all the mountains by ourselves. Our own sheer cunning is not enough when we have to deal with the world of disability. We cling to God, as we all should, because we have to. There is no other way. And we cling every day, hour by hour. We might not feel strong, but we are strong when we rely on God. As Philip Yancey observes,

> *We creatures, we jolly beggars, give glory to God*
> *by our dependence. Our wounds and defects are the*
> *very fissures through which grace might pass. It is our*
> *human destiny on earth to be imperfect, incomplete,*

weak, and mortal, and only by accepting that destiny can we escape the force of gravity and receive grace. Only then can we grow close to God.[4]

CHAPTER 8

The Language Barrier

*Undoubtedly, there are all sorts of
languages in the world,
yet none of them is without meaning.*
(1 COR. 14:10)

M ost every parent takes for it granted that one day their baby will speak. We're willing to endure months or even years of crying just to hear that first word, because it will usher in a whole new life for us. Finally, we'll be able to communicate more clearly—we won't have to face the frustration of not knowing what our child wants when he or she cries. People often think that mothers have a built-in "baby-cry translator," but I must confess that I didn't always do so well. When my infant sons cried inconsolably, I yearned for the gift of language. I wanted desperately to meet their needs. And I wanted to know what was going on inside their tiny heads—what were their dreams, their desires, their feelings?

Spoken language means emotional connection between parent and child. And often, it also grants a feeling of success as parents. We think that if our children aren't crying, they must be happy; and if our children are happy, then we're good parents. So the sooner we can stop our babies from screaming about everything, the sooner we can wear our "Good Mommy" and "Good Daddy" badges!

But what do we do when our children's disabilities prevent them from speaking, or when their disabilities themselves are language-based, like autism? It's easy to interpret their failure to gain language skills, which can be the first sign of their particular disabilities, as our failure to be good parents. It is challenging to learn that our worth doesn't come from the perceived happiness of our kids and that spoken language isn't the only way to communicate.

Quite a few years ago, a friend of mine accurately observed that it must be particularly difficult for me to not be able to talk to my kids because I love to talk so much! It was painful for me because instead of clear meaning we had misunderstandings, and instead of speech we had tears. I knew my children's lack of communication skills was not their fault, especially after discovering the extent of their disabilities. But it was a frustrating barrier. Whenever my sons tried to communicate and I couldn't understand them, I felt stupid. I kept thinking that, as their mother, I should be wise enough to catch a clue as to what they wanted. "Do you want something to eat? No? A toy? Something to drink? How about a nap . . . Please?" The more they tried to make themselves known, the more confused I became—which made them more frustrated in turn. In those early years, everyone in our house lived with a certain level of mystery.

To solve some of these mysteries of communication, my sons needed to learn a new way of speaking, and my husband and I had to learn a new way of listening. In this process, I came to understand that there are many languages, and none are without meaning.

How Language Happens

The way children learn language really is amazing. A few years ago, the local PBS station aired a series on language development in which a variety of linguists and experts in communication were interviewed. The thing that struck me was the assertion that most of us have a built-in "language decoder." People generally just start talking, because that's what we're "programmed" to do. They found that most three year olds know how to correct themselves grammatically, even though no one has taught them how. This occurs in every language on earth, no matter how complicated the grammar. In other words, for a typical human being, proper language just happens. When you think about how hard it is to learn a foreign language, you'll see how truly mind-boggling this is!

Since language usually comes so easily, we take it for granted. But when we understand how much goes into effective communication, we gain a greater appreciation for this gift God has given us. We may also learn new communication skills when our children speak to us in ways that don't use audible words.

What exactly is language? It is a code in which specific symbols stand for something else, and these symbols must be agreed upon in a community in order for the code to make sense. Rules governing language must be learned so that we can understand when to say what and to whom.

A comedian once had a routine in which he pondered what it would be like if adults taught kids how to speak the wrong way. Wouldn't it be funny, he thought, if instead of calling objects by their proper names, we labeled them incorrectly? A phone would be a chair; a dog would be table, and so forth. The comedian asked the audience to imagine the child's first sentence: "Kitty fat dog banana." This brought peals of laughter, but it isn't so funny to those whose children actually have a language disorder. It does, however, reinforce the fact that everyone must agree that a phone is indeed called a phone, and a chair is called a chair.

According to the resourceful text, *An Introduction to Children with Language Disorders* by Vickie A. Reed, language contains several components:

• phonology—how sounds are made,
• semantics—what something means,
• syntax—a set of rules that govern how words are related, and
• pragmatics—the use of language for achieving communication and social connection.

We can teach our children all the words in the dictionary, but if they can't use them properly, it's all for nothing.

Pragmatics are the rules that allow for proper communication—rules such as taking turns in conversation, appropriately reading and sending nonverbal cues, and providing adequate information to the listener. Have you ever had a "conversation" with someone who wouldn't stop talking? Despite your cues—looking at your watch, sighing heavily, looking past the speaker, passing out—the person never picked up on the fact that you were through listening. Aside from being told, "Look, you're a windbag; be quiet," some people never notice that others aren't listening to them anymore. That's a breach of pragmatics.

Pragmatics also includes the listener's ability to repair communication when it breaks down by being able to request additional information to clarify the message. Sometimes a person will say something that makes no sense to us. If we aren't capable of asking the proper questions to get the information we need, the speaker can go on for hours and still not tell us what we need to know.

When Language Doesn't Happen

Our children with special needs often have a variety of neurological anomalies that impede their ability to speak as typical children do. They may have oral-motor problems caused by cerebral palsy, Down syndrome, a stroke, or verbal dyspraxia. Forming the sounds orally may take more muscle control than they have. They may possess the mental ability to formulate language, but getting it out may prove difficult, if not impossible. We've all heard stories about people who were mistakenly thought to have mental retardation because of their inability to speak. But when an alternate mode of communication was used, it was discovered that these people were not only mentally sound but were indeed brilliant. How frustrating to have your thoughts locked inside your head! For many children and their families, though, this is reality.

Families of children with limited or nonexistent verbal skills face a tremendous challenge. The language barrier makes the day-to-day operations of feeding and toileting that much more difficult. While there are other methods of communicating, such as gestures and facial expressions, these usually convey only the broadest sense of language. Parents can usually tell if their child is angry or happy, but what about all the in-between emotions: irritation, anxiety, or just plain funky? These can all be mistaken for other emotions. And guessing the cause of these moods can be like playing twenty questions. Are our children irritated because a molar is coming in, or their stomach doesn't feel well, or simply because it's Tuesday?

Some parents have to become experts at reading their child's face or become more aware of the child's habits and emotional cycles. Some become experts at their child's different utterances; much like a new mother learns to interpret the tone of her baby's cries. For some families, technology in the form of augmentative communication (electronic voice output devices) can be of help. These often cost too much for the average family to afford, though, like other auxiliary equipment such as motorized wheelchairs. Depending on a family's situation, sometimes insurance or state agencies can help defer the cost.

Maybe your child doesn't have an oral-motor problem but a type of processing disorder—-his or her ears work just fine, but the spoken word travels up that auditory path and gets lost up there somewhere. Our son Daniel was a facially expressive child and often used grand gestures during his attempts at speaking. His language was a very guttural one, yet it sounded meaningful. Strangers often thought he was speaking German, and with his Teutonic looks he could have fooled anyone but a native of Germany. Once someone thought he was fluent in Japanese! It got so frustrating for him at one point that he basically quit trying to talk altogether. We got him into speech therapy by the time he was four years old and were told that his central auditory processing disorder was making it difficult for him to interpret the sounds he heard into what he used to make words. The situation reminded me of the sounds those unseen adults on the Peanuts television specials make, "Mwah, mwah-mwah." I wondered if that's what we sounded like to Daniel. No wonder he couldn't communicate effectively; to him everyone must have sounded like they were speaking with their hands cupped over their mouths.

If your child has autism, you know that I cannot possibly explain in one paragraph the mystery of language, or the lack of it, in these special children. Can children with autism speak, or do they choose not to? If they do not learn to speak by the age of six, which experts conclude is the cutoff point for language acquisition, does that mean they will never speak? Why do some children with autism go on to gain great verbal skills while some remain communicatively challenged? And if a child gains speech, does that mean he will be able to master pragmatics and actually be able to communicate?

A higher intelligence level seems to aid in language acquisition for the child with autism, but it is often difficult to discern that level without verbal skills. Vocalizing words and putting them together in a sentence that makes sense are two different things, and the latter is something that sometimes eludes those with autism. Occasionally, they will use too many words, often about topics nobody cares about or that people consider odd. This more often drives people away than promotes social intimacy. Most people don't want to talk at length about vacuum cleaners or all the wooden roller coasters in North America. Obsessing on these topics tends to lower a child's chance at keeping friends. Often, when a child with autism enters a program, it is hard to predict what the outcome will be because each child's experience with autism is individual.

What Can We Do?

How does a parent cope with a language barrier? We must learn how to communicate in a different manner from most of the people around us. We have a variety of possible ways to listen and make ourselves understood to our children. The important thing to do is discover what those ways are. Research your child's particular disability; talk to other parents about methods that worked for them. And pray for wisdom and understanding.

My husband and I discovered that our boys responded strongly to visual aids. Picture books (when they were old enough not to rip the pages out) and educational videos were things that held their interest. Because both of them have what are known as "perseverative" traits—they tend to exhaust one topic at a time, like an "idea binge"—we used that to our advantage. Did they like trains? We checked out every train book from the library, bought others, watched every train video, went to train museums, bought every Thomas the Train toy and related paraphernalia. There is not one train or railroad system in North America and Europe that we didn't read about. While I am now completely sick of trains, I have to admit that trains were great teaching aids. We started with simple pictures of trains, labeling each of the parts, saying the names very slowly and deliberately. We repeated everything...a lot.

As our boys gained a few more language skills, we started working on a few more complex sentences. We read out loud a lot. Not that the kids understood what we were saying, but we made it a habit, and we made sure lots of interesting pictures supplemented the reading. Keeping them from ripping out the pages when they were younger was a challenge; we didn't let them near library books for that reason. But when they showed they would not damage the books, we started taking them for very short trips to the library. They were allowed to pick out any three books they wanted. They couldn't necessarily read, but they could look at the pictures and be exposed to the words.

The books the boys picked out were always on the same topics. When Daniel got burned out on trains, he explored every single book in the entire library on dinosaurs and other prehistoric creatures. Jonathan read every book in the library on the solar system. At age five, he couldn't answer a question like, "How was your day at school today?" but he could name all the planets, tell how many moons each of them have, and most of the moons' corresponding names. Now he can answer how his day at school was, name the planets, but he can't name their corresponding moons. I find this interesting, because I am noting that as Jonathan gains more skills verbally and socially, he seems to be losing a lot of what I consider his photographic memory.

We also asked our sons' teachers what methods they were using at school to teach communication skills and tried to do the same thing at home. Jonathan's speech teacher, Miss Trisha, used little picture cards to be able to communicate with him. These cards are often used with children with autism because these kids respond especially well to visual aids. Miss Trisha made a lot of her cards on the computer, some of them in color, some of them black-and-white line drawings. They pictured objects you would find at home, in the classroom, and in the world at large. Each drawing had a simple word in lowercase letters written above or below it, identifying what the object was. Because children with autism respond best to concrete ideas, labeling items is a good way to go. It also helps if the drawings are consistent—your picture of a table at home needs to look the same as the picture at school. Children with autism don't deal well with inconsistencies. If the child has no verbal language at all, a notebook with small picture cards can be set up so the child can point to the pictures to communicate his or her needs. The picture cards can also be set up around the class or home so the child can point to the item he or she wishes and, if possible, say the word while touching the picture.

When Jonathan first entered his special day class, his teachers had a variety of these cards set up around the room. Some were pictures of food, some were pictures of the playground, and one was a picture of a toilet. The children were required to touch the picture before they went outside for recess, had their lunch, or used the bathroom. If you have a child with autism, you know that what one parent posted on the internet is true: "It's not just toilet-training; it's a way of life."

Nobody was making much progress with our younger son in this area. Since he wasn't effective verbally, my husband and I really didn't know what upset him about the toilet. And we couldn't figure out why he insisted on hitting the left side of the door frame before he entered the toilet area. We finally asked the teacher, and she explained that at school they had a picture of the toilet on the left side of the door frame of the bathroom. When we did the same at home, and when Jonathan hit the door frame, it made sense to him. Eventually he was able to say toilet, and after a year and a half of diligent work, he was actually able to use it. The toilet picture is very significant to me, because this self-help skill was a major milestone that I've never taken for granted. If you come to my house, you'll find I still have the toilet card hanging in our office. And now you'll know why.

Even with picture cards or electronic keyboards, sometimes we simply don't know what our children want. We don't know if they are not hungry because their stomachs hurt or because they're just full. We don't know if they look listless because they're ill or because they're just bored. Some things we can't figure out, so we have to make some assumptions. We have to assume that our children really do desire to connect with us, even if they can't say it. And we also have to not make assumptions. We cannot assume that our children, when they are cranky and whine and moan, are out to get us. (Even though there are days when it feels like that.)

One of the biggest assumptions I have made with my children is that they love me. If you have a child with autism, you know that this is a large and vital assumption, because a child with autism does not, in general, say he loves people. And a child with autism does not always recognize his own parents or understand who they are. Even though I wasn't sure if one of my sons knew me as his mother—he chose not to acknowledge my presence most of the time, and when he began to verbally address me, he always called me Michelle because that's what my husband calls me—I assumed he knew who I was. That might have been a false assumption at the time! But you have to do these things, or the language barrier seems insurmountable and you begin to resent it more than you already do.

We will never really know all that goes on inside our child's head. It would be nice to have a computer readout of everything that goes on inside our child's brain, don't you think? Maybe then we'd know why they refused to let us put their shoes on or why they cried when we brought them their favorite meal. But we probably won't know this side of Paradise what really goes on inside the mind of our child. Only God knows what is in our hearts and minds, and I believe that occasionally He does give us insight into our child's behaviors, if we ask Him.

Even if God refuses to enlighten us on our child's thoughts, though, it does not stop us from caring for our child with special needs. We would change the diaper, whether our child could ask us to or not. We would administer the proper medications, we would clean the feeding tube, and we would try to soothe the tears, because this is our job and we love our child. Our life would be a little less strained if we had more language to communicate, but it couldn't make us love our child any more than we do. This is a glimpse of unconditional love—mere words cannot increase it. The barrier between our child and us is simply a barrier of the mind, not of the heart.

The same type of barriers can exist in our relationship with the Lord as well. We don't always understand what goes on in the mind of God; because God Himself says His ways are so much higher than our ways (Isa. 55:8—9). Yes, it's frustrating when we don't completely understand our circumstances or when the Bible passage we read makes no sense to us at all. Or when our prayers seem misunderstood or misinterpreted. Sometimes our language skills with God seem to be lacking something. But, it sure doesn't stop Him from loving us, and it shouldn't stop us from loving Him. Maybe we have to make assumptions about God as well. Maybe we have to assume that He hears us and cares immensely for us and is working diligently even when we don't sense it. Romans 8:25—28 says:

If we hope for what we do not yet have, we wait for it patiently.

In the same way, the Spirit helps us in our weakness. We do not know what we ought to pray for, but the Spirit himself intercedes for us with groans that words cannot express. And he who searches our hearts knows the mind of the Spirit, because the Spirit intercedes for the saints in accordance with God's will.

And we know that in all things God works for the good of those who love him, who have been called according to his purpose.

As frustrating as this language barrier is, hang tough; it won't be this way forever. One day, in heaven, the veil will be lifted. The barriers of language and the barriers of misunderstanding will be demolished. Articulation will be perfect, no words will be wasted, and everyone will have strong clear voices. Our children will have perfect language, and so will we. Perfect language is necessary for one thing: to praise God in all eternity. Only one type of obsessive monologue will be allowed, that which praises the Creator. No one in heaven will be without words, as the book of Revelation describes:

Then I heard what seemed to be the voice of a great multitude, like the sound of many waters and like the sound of mighty thunderpeals, crying out,

"Hallelujah!

*For the Lord our God the Almighty reigns.
Let us rejoice and exult and give him the glory."
(19:6—7a NRSV)*

CHAPTER 9

Alienation and Judgment: Challenges in Our Quest to Belong

*I have become estranged from my brothers
And an alien to my mother's sons.*
(Ps. 69:8)

I would bet that most of us, at some point in life, have strived to fit in, to belong, to carve out a comfortable niche within a group of similar friends. As kids, being different made us a target for teasing or exclusion—whether our difference consisted of not wearing the "right" clothes, not having the "in" hairstyle, not being up on the cool music, or wearing braces, glasses, or special shoes. Nobody wanted to be branded with the dreaded "W" word: weirdo! Like lemmings, most of us rushed headlong to blend in with everybody else. Sameness meant safety, even if our individuality was headed over a cliff.

Now that we have a child with special needs, however, there's no more blending in with the crowd. Instead, crowds sometimes part when they see us coming. People's stares and whispers force us out of our comfortable anonymity and into an unaccustomed and unforgiving spotlight. Our life's efforts to blend in safely have been stripped away, leaving us exposed and shivering.

As much as we may sometimes want to, there's no going back to our old secure way of life. Instead, we need to keep moving forward, learning to cope with and accept our feelings of alienation and being different, as well as to deflect and forgive the hurtful judgments of others. It takes a lot of grace and perseverance to be different and still belong, but with God's help, we can do it.

The Winding Paths of Alienation

Have you ever been out shopping, surrounded by other people, and suddenly felt like you just sprouted antennas? As you and your special child moved past people, an eerie hush fell, and eyes either opened wide or darted away. Being a parent of a child with special needs is a surefire way to feel like you've been dropped off the mother ship into alien territory.

Even when our children are not visibly different, our parenting experience often wildly diverges from that of parents of typical children. "Two roads diverged in a yellow wood," wrote Robert Frost, and God has set us on the path "less traveled by"[1] —the path of disability and all that it entails.

Take something as basic as potty-training, for example. Most parents have triumphed over dirty diapers by the time their child enters preschool. But some of us are still dealing with Pampers in elementary school, and some never finish with diapers.

Or think about family activities. Many parents spend a lot of time, energy, and money nurturing their children's interests and talents—art, dance, and music lessons, as well as sports. Every day you see moms and dads rushing around town in cars, vans, and SUVs ferrying their children to their multitude of activities. The back window of the vehicle is sometimes full of stickers proclaiming milestones the children have reached; honor roll, all-star team or both. If our children are functional enough, we may be able to participate in some of these activities too. But usually, when families with children with disabilities rush around in cars, vans, and SUVs they're going to the doctor, the therapist, or the emergency room. Too bad they don't make bumper stickers to reflect our kids' accomplishments: "My Child Is a Star at Metropolitan Hospital" or "Honk If You Love Occupational Therapy"!

Now, of course, we share many similarities with parents of typical children. We both love our kids very much. We both must attend to our kids' many needs. We both hope that our children will reach their highest potential. But we do travel several different paths that set us apart and can make us feel strange: the paths of being different, of needing special equipment, and of having to medicate our child.

The Path of Being Different

Parents of children with severe disabilities often face discrimination because their children look different. They don't walk like other children. They don't talk like other children. They may have unusual behaviors, like hand-flapping or rocking or squealing and screaming. If they have a chromosomal abnormality or congenital malformations, they don't look like other children either.

Most people have no idea how much it hurts to have others turn away when our child comes by. Perhaps people feel afraid or don't know what to do, but it still feels like the ultimate rejection as a parent. We wish others knew our children as we know them. We also wish we saw more children like ours in a public setting so we wouldn't feel so alone. "Where are they?" "Why are we the only ones here?" We may not be the only ones there; quite possibly, other children with disabilities are nearby, but they just don't look disabled.

Those of us who have children with less visible disabilities can feel caught between two worlds, and on some days, we feel like we don't belong to either. Our children may not have any physical markers—no wheelchair, no telltale gait, no different facial features. Instead, they learn differently, play differently, and speak differently from other children. They may be particularly adept at one skill and completely lacking in another. They may lack social skills, causing others brand them as difficult, ill behaved, or defiant. They may feel compelled to wash obsessively, count repeatedly, and make vocal tics. Well past the age of social acceptability, our children may tantrum when upset, cry huge tears when disappointed, or laugh uncontrollably at situations that aren't really funny. They may not be able to sit still, go to sleep, or pay attention.

But they look like typical children, so people who don't know them expect them to behave like typical children. They aren't, though. They may not be able to keep up in the classroom without special help. They may not be able to catch and hit the ball without extra coaching, let alone spur their baseball team on to victory.

As parents, we want to shield our kids from impatient teachers and coaches, but we also don't want to stigmatize our kids by labeling them up front. Should we tell the coach? Or should we see how it goes—wait until things fall apart and then try to explain what obsessive compulsive disorder is? We stand on the sidelines, holding our breath and clenching our fists, hoping our kids don't act up. And sometimes it doesn't matter if we explain our children's special needs anyway; we are often met with blank stares. "They don't look like they have special needs." We can only imagine what others think—or sometimes people spell out their judgments for us: "Must be bad parenting."

No, our kids may not look different, but they see the world differently—and they make us see it differently too. We can no longer assume that everyone basically thinks the same, because we know our kids do not. On the positive side, they open our eyes to all the differences around us. We don't view things as black and white anymore; we see all the shades and nuances of gray. When someone else's child shouts and cries and wrestles in a tantrum, for example, "Brat!" isn't the first idea that comes to mind now. Instead, we look more carefully and see a child who just might face some of the challenges our children face.

On the negative side, however, we see just how unprepared the world is to accommodate those with special needs and different ways of relating.

The Path of Special Equipment

The practicalities of moving through life with a child who needs constant care are even more alienating. You are limited in where you can go, how you spend your free time (if there is any), and how others accept you and your child. Those with children who have severe disabilities struggle daily with physical, emotional, and often financial exhaustion.

In many ways, it is like caring for an elder who has lost the ability to care for himself or herself. You must build safeguards into your home and make sure a responsible adult constantly monitors your child's needs and well-being. One family I know had to move from a two-story apartment to a one-story when it became more difficult to carry their little girl up and down the stairs. Getting the carrier or wheelchair into the car and then out again is a challenge, as is getting the child in and out of the carrier or wheelchair. And there's always the realization that at some point, it may take two of you to move your child. There's nothing more isolating than being at home with a child who is non-ambulatory and realizing that it would be difficult, if not impossible, to run an emergency errand.

Most parents don't have to think of these things, or at least not for any length of time. True, when our children were young, we had cumbersome strollers, diapers, bottles, baby food, and all that stuff. Do you remember what a drag it was to lug it all around? Going to the store was not an errand; it was a juggernaut! And what about the toddler years? The screaming, temper tantrums, toilet training, and messes. It seemed as though something—sometimes everything—was always sticky. And who doesn't have stories involving small inanimate objects and body cavities, or medium-sized inanimate objects and plumbing?

Now, if you are the parent of a typical child, imagine that your child will never developmentally outgrow infant or toddler stage. For some parents, this is their life. Most people cannot relate to this and do not know how to handle a child so different from their own.

The Path of Medication

The choices we have to make for our special children also differ, sometimes dramatically, from those of parents with typical children. One such choice is whether to medicate our kids. Often, this is a choice we do not even want to make. If it was a matter of our child's physical well-being, the choice would not be so difficult—it would seem as obvious as healing an infection with antibiotics or treating asthma with an inhaler. But our choices often involve our child's mental, emotional, and social well being, and that's where the issue of medication becomes difficult.

Should we medicate our children to help them function? Will a pill make my child sit still so he can learn better? Will a tablet make my daughter stop washing her hands over and over again so that she can actually go out and play? Will medication lessen my son's tics so people won't make fun of him?

Many of us who parent children with special needs have had to face these questions. Personally, I dislike having to medicate my child. Some of the side effects are almost more frightening than the symptoms we're seeking to treat. But my husband and I see medication as a tool to give our child every advantage possible.

There's nothing more alienating, however, than trying to explain to confused friends and family why you've given your child medications that are often reserved for the adult population.

Have you ever noticed that people who have never needed to give psychotropic medications to their children are the first to hand you magazine articles denouncing them? Or they offer this bit of help: "Oh, you give your child a stimulant? How sad! That's terrible! Is there anything else you can do?" What can we say to that? Most of us have prayed diligently about this matter and explored every other option, such as diets and behavioral techniques, only to find that our children still need the additional boost of medication.

One of the medications we give our older son requires that a tablet be cut into quarters (it's already the smallest dose available). I have a pill cutter, so normally chopping pills into quarters would not be a problem, but these pills are so small that they are reduced to little shards and piles of medication dust. Administering these shards at home isn't a problem; I can keep track of which piece goes with which piece, but at school it's a problem.

Our school district policy dictates that the medication be stored in the original container in the dosage prescribed. The school is not allowed to cut the pills, so they require that I cut them up, place the shards and powder in small pieces of foil, and then stuff them in the container. You haven't experienced the Twilight Zone unless you've spent the evening watching TV and cutting up tiny white pills with a pill cutter and pouring the contents into little foil packets. The whole time I'm thinking the

Drug Enforcement Agency is ready to burst through the door, guns drawn. "What's with the white powder, ma'am? And the foil packets?" Or the D.A.R.E. officer at my sons' school is peering through the window and shouting, "What did we teach you, son—'Just say "no" to drugs!'" Well, yes, unless your mommy gives them to you.

It's just not the same as giving your child an aspirin. It's much weirder and much more complicated. I definitely don't feel like other moms when I survey our pill collection. And I don't think anybody else understands my odd sense of humor when I deadpan, "Hey, I'm an advocate of better living through pharmaceuticals." From the icy stares of others, to the lectures from them on chemical poisoning, I sometimes feel like I'm on my own planet. And I don't expect anyone else to understand unless they've handed their child a glass of water, a pill, and said, "Swallow." It's hard.

The Treacherous Cliffs of Judgment

As if alienation weren't bad enough, the judgments of others can pitch us right over an emotional cliff. Some people, and certainly not all—there are a lot of kind, compassionate, and helpful people in this world—communicate a cruel message with just a look: You don't belong here. You shouldn't be out in public. This certainly happens when the person's disability is physically visible, but it's sometimes done even more harshly when the disability reveals itself only in behavior. And, sadly, judgment comes not only from the general public but also from those within the disabled community.

Judgment from "Outsiders"

Sometimes judgments unnerve us through a silent, piercing look, a roll of the eyes, or a click of the tongue. Other times we reel from a frontal assault—when someone decides to tell us what they think...whether we want to know or not.

I remember an incident from a few years back that perhaps you can identify with. Now, some people believe that they've been "touched by an angel", but on this day, I believe I was touched by something else.

My sons and I had spent a long morning in the local Target store. The kids were worn out, and I could tell that if we didn't leave soon, one or both of them would "derail"—-their emotional "train" would jump the track with a loud, and sometimes violent, temper tantrum. (Autism is fun that way, you never really know when and where and at what velocity a major outburst will occur.) To avoid a scene, we would need to dash to the car—- immediately—-and then thank my van's manufacturer for soundproofing. But time ran out, and unfortunately, we crashed and burned in the main aisle on the way to the express checkout.

As I sat sprawled in the aisle, trying to keep my younger son from splitting his skull on the floor in a head-banging tantrum, I could feel my face turn as red as our little shopping basket. It took everything in me to hold my son's head above the ground, and I slipped my hands under his head to let my fingers take the brunt of his banging. Because I had to let go of my older son, he "eloped" (a poetic term given to the behavior of "running away" which is common to those with autism) to the clothes racks in the adjacent children's section.

I must have looked pathetic, fighting with a very strong and agitated three year old and hissing at my six year old, "Get back over here! Now!" The little red basket got knocked over in the scuffle, so with my third invisible arm I tried to retrieve the rolling items. Quite a few folks were watching this scene. Unfortunately, none of them included my children.

Then, out of the corner of my eye, I noticed an elderly gentleman by the jewelry section taking great pains, shuffling and limping along, to make it over to where I was splayed out. Could it be? Someone to help me? This poor man was working so hard to get to me. What a guy!

When he finally arrived, he bent down and uttered in the most disgusted tone I had heard in a long time, "If those were my kids, I'd smack 'em!" Then he turned slowly and painfully around and shuffled back to the jewelry section. I remember thinking that I was glad they weren't his kids.

This wasn't the first time someone had lent me a bit of "advice," but usually they were stuck somewhere in line behind me or seated nearby in a fast food restaurant. Nobody had ever specifically gone out of his or her way to spit venom at me. If I hadn't been so shocked, I probably would have cried. Years later, I still marvel at the man's tenacity to put a total stranger in her place. He probably burned up the last of his arthritis medication in his effort to deliver his "counsel."

Why would he do such a thing? Why would he make such a labored journey to exhale three seconds' worth of noxious judgment? I don't know. Perhaps Satan was egging him on— our enemy delights in tearing us apart with shame and humiliation (after all, his name in Hebrew means "adversary" and "accuser"). Whatever the case, I do know that criticism, disapproving looks, and harsh, uninformed advice are all part of our lot in life.

It doesn't make much sense, does it? You would think that compassion and mercy would be the more frequent responses to people so obviously in need. Thankfully, sometimes others do approach us and our children that way. But many do not. Perhaps fear drives some of the nondisabled community to act as they do —fear of what our child might do, fear of the disability itself, fear of becoming disabled themselves through accident or disease.

For the angry and toxic people, though, the issue is probably more about control than fear, especially when our children have behavior-oriented disabilities—such as obsessive-compulsive disorder, autism, and Tourette syndrome. Many who are unfamiliar with these disabilities may simply look at us and see parents who can't control their children and who aren't teaching them any manners. To them, the issue is simple: stronger discipline.

We'll never be immune to the stinging judgments of others, but we won't always be taken completely off guard by it. Realizing that the non-disabled community often simply doesn't understand what's going on with our children can help. We can learn to extend patient grace in the face of ignorance. We can stand strong in the truth of what we know about our children. And we can gently assuage people's fears by teaching them that our children have dignity and worth. In short, we can deflect some of the hurt of judgment by enlightening those who don't understand disability.

But how do we deal with the judgments from those who do understand—those from within the community of disability itself?

Judgment from "Insiders"

At a conference on autism, my mother and I shared a table with another family. We introduced ourselves with friendly small talk, and then they asked a certain question: "Are you doing 'the therapy'?" This particular therapy was both well known and controversial, involving many hours of intensive training for the child. The therapy was also administered by a privately paid therapist who was schooled in the method. These two components of "the therapy" added up to a big investment in money and time. But a number of books promoted it, and some even touted it as a miracle cure.

My husband and I had explored this therapy briefly but decided not to pursue it. I was already too overwhelmed by caring for two children with differing special needs to be able to take this on as well. The prospect of having to work intensively eight hours a day for the next several months or possibly years was beyond my emotional scope at that time.

So I smiled at our tablemates and said, "No, we have our child in a special day class through our school district." At this, their faces fell. We sat at the table with them for the remainder of the day, but they never spoke to us again. Their silent withdrawal communicated a distinct message: they thought I was a negligent parent for not trying to cure my son's autism their way.

Judgment from within the community of disability usually blindsides us, doesn't it? We expect greater understanding from those who share similar struggles with us, who have to cope with the same sense of alienation. Yet it happens, perhaps regarding a therapy we follow or don't follow medications we use or forgo, or decisions to keep a child at home or place him or her elsewhere.

What are the effects of these judgments? They wither our confidence and hope. We start to doubt our ability to make wise decisions for our children, and we despair of ever making their lives better. In his book <u>Guilt and Grace</u>, doctor and counselor Paul Tournier titles one of his chapters "Judgment Is Destructive," explaining that it crushes our spirits and more:

> *Other people's judgment exercises a paralysing*
> *effect. Fear of criticism kills spontaneity; it prevents men*

*from showing themselves and expressing themselves
freely, as they are. . . .*
*. . This fear of being criticized impoverishes
mankind. It is the source of all the conformism which
levels men and locks them away in impersonal modes
of behavior. How many very sensitive authors have
never dared to face public criticism and have locked
their masterpieces away?*[2]

And how many compassionate, committed parents of
children with disabilities have isolated themselves, too afraid of
being attacked or rejected by others' judgments to get the
support they need or can give? Even though we're Christians,
we're still human——and that means we're still made of flesh and
blood that bruises and bleeds.

What can we do to hold onto our confidence and hope in
the face of disapproval from within our own community?
Tournier offers some encouraging insights:

*The Bible is a school of courage: courage to
recognize our wrongdoings; courage also, at times, to
stand by our convictions unflinchingly. . . .*
*For the Bible also lays upon us the duty of defending
ourselves, of not allowing ourselves to be crushed by
the judgment of others, by the constant pretension of
others to take our place as judges of our conduct and
to exercise a moral oversight of our life. In our turn we
are called to observe the same reserve towards other
people, to resist setting ourselves up as judges of other
people's conduct.*[3]

No one has a right to judge. Remember what Jesus told us,
"Don't pick on people, jump on their failures, criticize their
faults——unless, of course, you want the same treatment. That
critical spirit has a way of boomeranging. . . . It's this whole
traveling road-show mentality all over again, playing a holier-
than-thou part instead of just living your part" (Matt. 7:1—2, 5 THE
MESSAGE).[4] Jesus never caved in to the merciless judgments of
the Pharisees; instead, He repeatedly tried to teach them the
error of their judgmental ways. We need to learn from His
strength——and ask for His strength——to take courage and stand

strong in the truth. And courage, by the way, is not the absence of fear but "the attitude of facing and dealing with anything recognized as dangerous, difficult, or painful, instead of withdrawing from it."[5]

We also need Jesus' help to not turn on others in judgment. It's easy to become resentful and defensive, bitter about continually being judged by those inside and outside the community of disability. From there, it's a small step to becoming judgers ourselves. We can jump to conclusions about others' looks or remarks, ready to pounce with a counterattack on those who had no attack in mind. And we can complete the cycle of judgmental misery by criticizing other parents, both those who have children with special needs and those who don't.

As the Lord Himself has shown us, the remedy to judgment is grace. Grace to accept people where they are, as they are. Grace to not retaliate but extend understanding and forgiveness. Grace to recognize that the Lord is at work in each of our lives and to leave all judging with Him. Grace to "'ask ourselves, not whether what we say to someone is well-founded or not, but whether it is constructive or destructive for him'"[6] (see Eph. 4:29). Grace to know that we and our children are dearly loved and looked after by God Himself.

Where judgment kills the spirit, grace brings it to life (see Eph. 2:4—8). And one of the best things we can do to cope with judgment and the ensuing alienation is to gather regularly with grace-oriented people who travel the same path we do.

Finding Travelers on the Same Path

By nature, we human beings search for a group or a place in which we feel understood, appreciated, and heard. I have been fortunate to find such a group at my church. It's made up primarily of moms of kids with special needs to give them a night out for fun. My friend Gayle wrote our mission statement:

> Our group is an opportunity for mothers (and other caregivers) of children with special needs to come together for a relaxing, fun, enjoyable experience; and even if for an hour, set our worries aside. We want to be

uplifting and encouraging. Our common thread is that all of our children have delay difficulties or disabilities of some nature. Because of this, we all have burdens to carry. Some are greater than others. Let us be careful not to engage in contests of hardships, as no one is the winner of such things. While concerns may be shared, we wish our times together to be ones of encouragement to all.

We sent out cards announcing our first meeting, and we started a newsletter to keep those moms who couldn't come informed of upcoming events and news pertaining to disability. Several members attend other churches, and we always hope that they feel the love of Christ when they enter our meetings. We try to have time to share a little about our families, and then we eat and do some networking.

One of the greatest benefits of coming together is the tacit understanding of the difficulties we as parents with special children face. When someone tells about a frustrating experience regarding a medical procedure or a special education meeting that didn't go well, you can see heads bob up and down in agreement. "Yes, we know what you feel." When someone tells of the fears they have for their child's future, you can hear other moms murmur, "Yes, we understand."

It's such a relief to share an experience that you felt was off-the-wall and hear several people say, "Me too!" Moms feel less alienated at that moment. For a couple of hours every other month, we all have an opportunity to feel connected and safe. And that's priceless.

Some Thoughts for Our Journey

There's no way to neatly wrap up and tie a pretty ribbon on the messy issues of alienation and judgment. But in studying the Scriptures, I've found several strengths we can grab hold of from God's person and purposes.

First, God has great compassion for the alienated. His Law overflows with concern that the alien or stranger be treated justly, mercifully, and with love (see Exod. 22:21; 23:12; Lev. 19:10, 34; Num. 15:16; Deut. 26:12). The Lord has always had the outsider's best interests at heart—after all, we were outsiders, even enemies, and He nevertheless sent His Son to die for our sins and reconcile us to Himself. Through Christ, we've been brought in, into the very family of God. We can gather encouragement from this truth.

Second, in bringing we "who once were far away . . . near" (Eph. 2:13), Jesus experienced incredible alienation. John tells us that

> *Though the world was made through him, the world did not recognize him. He came to that which was his own, but his own did not receive him. (John 1:10—11)*

And the prophet Isaiah foretold that Jesus would be "despised and rejected by men . . . like one from whom men hide their faces" (Isa. 53:3). Many of our children can identify with this, and it breaks our hearts. Jesus knows. He was misunderstood by those who should have known Him best, let down by those He needed most, deserted by those closest to Him, and crucified by those who should have seen His identity the clearest. From these truths we can gather comfort.

Third, Jesus removed our alienation from God, but in another sense, we became alienated from the world around us. We live on earth, "but our citizenship is in heaven" (Phil. 3:20). We are "aliens and strangers in the world" (1 Pet. 2:11), and our real "life is now hidden with Christ in God" in heaven (Col. 3:3). So, even if we didn't have children with special needs, by virtue of being Christians we would still feel like aliens. As C. S. Lewis reminds us,

> *The settled happiness and security which we all desire, God withholds from us by the very nature of the world. . . . It is not hard to see why. The security we crave would teach us to rest our hearts in this world and [pose] an obstacle to our return to God: a few moments of happy love, a landscape, a symphony, a merry meeting with our friends, a [swim] or a football match have no such tendency. Our Father refreshes us on the journey with some pleasant inns, but will not encourage us to mistake them for home.[7]*

This reality gives us courage for our journey through this life.

Fourth, the Lord who compassionately cares for His aliens on earth is also a compassionate judge. Unlike critical people, who practically froth at the mouth when others do things differently from their way (the "right way"), God casts His judgments within the bounds of His holiness and love. Through the sacrifice of His Son, the Lord provided a way to be "just and the one who justifies those who have faith in Jesus" (Rom. 3:26). Frederick Buechner observes that "Christ's love so wishes our joy that it is ruthless against everything in us that diminishes our joy. . . . The one who judges us most finally will be the one who loves us most fully."[8]   This truth can anchor our hope.

And fifth, God's judgments are the only ones we really need to be concerned with, a fact that can give us great confidence. Let's take Eugene Peterson's rendering of Paul's thoughts in Galatians as our final word on this subject:

> *Make a careful exploration of who you are and the work you have been given, and then sink yourself into that. Don't be impressed with yourself. Don't compare yourself with others. Each of you must take responsibility for doing the creative best you can with your own life. . . .*
>
> *Don't be misled: No one makes a fool of God. What a person plants, he will harvest. The person who plants selfishness, ignoring the needs of others—ignoring God!—harvests a crop of weeds. All he'll have to show for his life is weeds! But the one who plants in response to God, letting God's Spirit do the growth work in him, harvests a crop of real life, eternal life.*
>
> *So let's not allow ourselves to get fatigued doing good. At the right time we will harvest a good crop if we don't give up, or quit. (Gal. 6:4—5, 7—9 THE MESSAGE)[9]*

CHAPTER *10*

We Have Work to Do (Part 1)

Be very careful, then, how you live—
not as unwise but as wise,
making the most of every opportunity,
because the days are evil.
(EPH. 5:15—16)

For hours, the young mother labored and pushed to deliver the baby she had fallen in love with months ago. Finally, the head was out, then the shoulders, and at last she could hold her new baby girl.

But the baby was whisked away. The exhausted mother only "caught a glimpse of the soft curve of her firstborn baby's bottom, nothing more." People were calling her baby a "monster" who was "too terrible for her parents to look at."

At the direction of the baby's grandfather, who was a prominent man in the city, the doctor told the grief-stricken parents, "Your wife gave birth to a monster, and this monster is in pain." She told them that it would not live long and the shorter time it lived the better. In most cases like this, she said, people give up babies like that.

What was wrong with the child? The doctor said she had a disability that prevented her from swallowing, from being able to bend her joints, and made one leg shorter than the other. Her heart had severe problems, her brain circulation was poor, and a large birthmark disfigured her face.

"Who needs a baby like that?" the doctor said. "Of course it was a freak. It looked terrible. None of the joints would bend. Just because the face looked OK doesn't mean it was not a monster."

And the grandfather lived near people whom he said "had a freak and it was in a wheelchair and looked like a monster. And for 30 years they went past my window, and I thought, 'Why should my children suffer like this?'"

Another doctor told the young mother that if she saw her "terrible-looking" baby, she would "never want to have a baby again." She finally learned of "her little girl's fate when a janitor told her to collect her things and move out of the maternity unit because her baby had died."

"I cried that I gave birth to a monster and now I had nothing," the mother said.

But was this baby a "monster"? Had she really died? Years later the mother learned that her father and the doctors had conspired to get rid of the disabled child. The tiny, vulnerable girl actually spent the first three years of her life in a baby home until she was adopted by a couple in another country.

The director of the baby home gave the mother a picture of her little girl at three years of age. With dark hair and bright eyes, the pretty little girl's smile shone from the photograph, piercing the heart of her confused and stunned mother.

There was no monster here, only a lively, intelligent, beautiful child with a disease called arthogryposis. With surgical help, the child could even walk.[1]

In what era do you think this terrible, true tale took place? Does it sound like something out of Dickens? Or maybe the early 1900s? Was it another atrocity of the Nazi era?

Try 1995. The doctor was a well-educated, powerful woman who, with her husband, the chief of the town's hospital, controlled access to health care in her region. The grandfather was a well-to-do, powerful police official at that time, and later took a respected government position.

The country this took place in was not a Third World nation ill-equipped to handle disability. It was Russia, a country proud of its scientific achievements.

Now, before we decide that this could never happen in America, let's think for a moment. Why do a lot of doctors not only recommend but pressure pregnant women to have an amniocentesis? Certainly it's to ensure the baby's well-being—but it's also done to see if the baby has Down syndrome or any other disability. As a result of the information gained, some parents are encouraged to and do choose to terminate their pregnancy.

This world system we live in does not place a high value on children who are different—who have special needs. But God does. And as His people, we have a lot of work to do to champion the precious lives and purposes God has for His special children.

In this chapter, we'll examine some of the attitudes and beliefs that devalue and even endanger our children. Then, in the next chapter, we'll take an in-depth look at God's heart and nature, learning from Him what we can and should do as a people called by His name.

What the World Sees

What do a lot of people in this world see when they look at our children? Often, they see a condition instead of a child— "He is retarded" . . . "She is blind" . . . "He is autistic" . . . "She is deformed" . . . "He is disabled." Rather than seeing a human being with a unique identity, many people view the disability as the identity. The person is the problem; there's no differentiation. This thinking boxes our children into all the things they can't do, as if their limitations defined them.

At a deeper (and perhaps barely conscious) level, people may see an inescapable reminder of their own limitations. So many of us strive to be strong, independent, self-sufficient—we take pride in our abilities, sometimes even honing them into weapons to conquer others in the battles of life. Yet not one of us is completely strong, independent, or self-sufficient. We all have areas of weakness, of dependence, of neediness. And though we spend a lifetime trying to deny they exist, they're with us when we wake up in the morning and when we go to bed at night.

Jesus addressed this false sense of self-sufficiency in the book of Revelation:

> *"These are the words of the Amen, the faithful and true witness, the ruler of God's creation. . . . You say, 'I am rich; I have acquired wealth and do not need a thing.' But you do not realize that you are wretched, pitiful, poor, blind and naked." (Rev. 3:14b, 17)*

We resist seeing our inner blindness, deafness, slowness, and weakness, don't we? We naturally look away from our emotional and spiritual shortcomings and needs, hoping that nobody else will notice them either.

As Christians, we know that humbly facing our own neediness is essential when we come to God for salvation and as we live the life He designed for us. "Blessed are the poor in spirit," Jesus told us, adding that "unless [we] change and become like little children, [we] will never enter the kingdom of heaven" (Matt. 5:3; 18:3).

The world, however, recoils from weakness and chases after power and perfection instead.

What are the outcomes of such a pursuit concerning those who have disabilities? One is eugenics—the desire to create perfection. A second is euthanasia—the attempt to eliminate imperfection. And a third is abuse—the drive to punish imperfection and need.

Eugenics: Creating Perfection

Eugenics, according to Microsoft Encarta, is "an outgrowth of the study of human heredity, aimed at 'improving' the genetic quality of the human stock."[2] The idea of perfecting the human race goes all the way back to Plato, but it gained new prominence with Charles Darwin's theories. In the late 1800s, social Darwinism took root in Western societies, suggesting "that the rich were better endowed than the poor and hence more successful in life" and promoting the idea that nature should take its course with poverty-stricken people "so that the worst elements of society would eventually be eliminated."[3] At its core, eugenics seeks to find biological solutions to perceived social problems.

Around 1900, with the advent of modern genetics, a more active eugenics approach developed in trying to better society through "proper breeding." Promoters of the eugenics movement advocated the breeding of superior individuals to improve society, focusing on those with especially high IQs, for example. Nazi Germany took this idea to a frightening new level and instituted it on a wide scale:

> *Hitler implemented programs aimed directly at middle-class families with the intent of stimulating fertility and enhancing the German germ plasm. To begin with, the Reich proscribed physicians from sterilizing, aborting, or providing birth control to healthy German women. . . . Local Nazi organizations mustered youth into race hygiene courses. . . .*
> *. . Here was eugenics in its most essential form being used to guide the future parents of a nation. . . . Medals [were] given out by the Nazis for extraordinary feats of motherhood. In the procreative Olympics, four children won you a bronze, six a silver, and eight a gold; eight being, apparently, the best effort the state could reasonably expect. . . . After World War II began, the Nazis in addition launched the Lebensborn (Well of life) scheme, whereby SS men were encouraged to impregnate as many single women as possible to increase the country's yield of children of "superior" genetic stock.[4]*

On the flip side of the "positive" aspect of eugenics policy lurked a "negative" approach: curtailing the breeding, often through sterilization, of less "fit" types of people, such as people with mental retardation, criminals, and those with mental illnesses.

The eugenics movement spread throughout the world, but it gained special strength and prominence in three countries. In England it was founded by Darwin's cousin, Sir Francis Galton, who hoped to improve humanity by having "'the more suitable races' prevail over 'the less suitable races.'"[5] In the United States, eugenics had made so much progress that by 1935, twenty-eight states had passed forced sterilization laws against people "incarcerated in state foster homes, mental institutions, or prisons" In California alone, somewhere between 12,941 and possibly 30,000 "defectives" were sterilized.[6] Finally, in Germany it reached a horrifying climax under eugenics devotee Adolf Hitler. According to <u>Victims of the Nazis: 1933—1945</u>,

> *Soon after Hitler took power, the Nazis formulated policy based on their vision of a biologically "pure" population, to create an "Aryan master race." The "Law for the Prevention of Progeny with Hereditary Diseases," proclaimed July 14, 1933, forced the sterilization of all persons who suffered from diseases considered hereditary, such as mental illness (schizophrenia and manic depression), retardation ("congenital feeble-mindedness"), physical deformity, epilepsy, blindness, deafness, and severe alcoholism.[7]*

People with disabilities were considered "inferiors" and "burdens on society." Propaganda films reinforced these attitudes by stressing how much caring for such people cost, as did school textbooks:

> *School mathematics books posed such questions as: "The construction of a lunatic asylum costs 6 million marks. How many houses at 15,000 marks each could have been built for that amount?"[7]*

Now, it's easy, too easy, to think, "Those Nazis were the epitome of evil! I'm glad we've seen the light and are past all that." But are we?

Some people are still trying to create superior people through selective breeding. In 1971, Robert K. Graham wrote a treatise on "improving the gene pool" titled <u>The Future of Man</u>, in which he hypothesized that humankind was faltering because "retrograde humans" were out-reproducing and outnumbering intelligent people. His answer to this "problem" was to create The Repository for Germinal Choice—a sperm bank holding the seed of Nobel Prize winners and young scientists to be used by young women of proven intelligence.

The Repository project began in the 1970s and ended in 1999, with the first baby from this program being born in 1982. By the time Graham died in 1997, 229 babies had been born.

Graham's theory was that these babies would grow up to be super-intelligent leaders and scientists who would change the world for the better. But he was never able to verify the results. When he mailed a survey to clients in the 1990s, most of them ignored it. Did these children turn out to be just like everybody else? Did they suffer from any pressure to become superstars? Did the parents learn that there is more to being a worthwhile human being than DNA alone?

And some still attach a price tag to human life. In 1996, the Task Force for U.S. Preventive Services published its second edition of <u>Guide to Clinical Preventive Services</u>, which listed the benefits of being able to screen for certain genetic anomalies. Recommendation 41, "Screening for Down Syndrome," begins with a section titled "Burden of Suffering" that estimates the "lifetime economic costs of Down syndrome" being $410,000 per case.[9]

What are the effects of a monetary "burden" figure being placed on a child with Down syndrome—or a child with any disability? Money certainly shapes attitudes. Some people think that money would be better spent elsewhere, say, on children who will be able to contribute to society rather than, in their view, drain it of its limited resources. Some parents may be scared off by the cost, not taking into consideration the degree of the disability—Down syndrome is not a cookie cutter that stamps each child the same.

And has anyone determined what the "lifetime economic costs" of raising a so-called normal child would be? It may be just as much or more, depending on that child's needs and talents, on any traumas or accidents he or she would encounter, on any sicknesses or special conditions that would develop, on the type of schooling as well as the choice of college.

We don't know what the future holds. We don't have total control over our lives or our children's lives. And genetics can't foretell the future or give us the control we crave.

But that still doesn't stop us. Take the screenings pregnant women can take to detect anything unusual in their pregnancies. (Let me just say from the outset that I'm not against these tests; they can be valuable helps in preparing a couple to care for a child with special needs.) For women over thirty-five, doctors recommend an amniocentesis or CVS (chorionic villus sampling), where a large needle is inserted into the woman's belly and into the womb to withdraw amniotic fluid. Doctors then analyze the fetal cells in the fluid, which can tell which sex the baby will be and if the baby has any chromosomal abnormalities or any problems with enzymes or growth. Women under thirty-five can take a less invasive screening—the maternal serum marker tests, which involve taking urine and/or blood to analyze the amount of human chorionic gonadotropin (HCG) or maternal serum alpha-fetoprotein (MSAFP).

In the state I live in, health care providers must offer by law Down syndrome screening. I was offered the serum tests during the fifth month of each of my pregnancies. Health care workers presented me with the paperwork explaining the tests, and I had to sign on the back sheet to confirm that I had, indeed, been offered the tests.

For personal reasons (especially my propensity to worry), I did not wish to take these tests. I did not trust their accuracy, and I knew I'd be upset and anxious the remainder of my pregnancy if I was told that my baby had chromosomal abnormalities. Abortion was not an option—carrying life, no matter what the baby's condition, was an awesome privilege to me. I decided that I would learn about any special needs my child might have on the delivery table and deal with them from there.

My health care providers—two different sets for each of my pregnancies—felt differently, however. They could not believe that I refused the tests. The second health care provider must have asked me five times if I was sure I knew what I was doing by refusing, "Nobody refuses the test. Are you sure you don't want peace of mind?"

I wonder what this person meant by "peace of mind"—assurance that my baby was fine, or opportunity to retain a "normal" life by aborting a child with special needs?

In the book *Genetic Ethics: Do the Ends Justify the Genes?*, Hessel Bouma III tells the story of Mr. and Mrs. Smith, who learned in the fourth month of pregnancy through a maternal serum test that their unborn child had a severe disorder—Trisomy 18. Instead of having two copies of chromosome 18, their baby boy had three, which would result in "severe malformations, significant mental impairments, and average life expectancy of six months."[10]   His head was four times the size it should have been, and his stomach was outside his abdomen. The doctor urged them to have an abortion immediately.

The Smiths, however, after praying about what to do and asking their church to pray too, decided not to terminate the pregnancy. When they told the doctor and his staff, they reacted with disapproval, were curt with them, and seemed "even full of ugly feelings and hate." Thankfully, as the pregnancy progressed, the staff softened and reluctantly came to appreciate "the Smith's commitment to their unborn child even at considerable inconvenience, expense, and substantial risk to Mrs. Smith's health." Born prematurely in the seventh month, the baby boy lived one hour, cradled by people who loved him.[11]

Like the Smiths, one woman I know personally has endured open hostility by those who question the sanity of knowingly bringing into this world a child with possible chromosomal abnormalities. Some have challenged her "moral authority" to "impose upon society" an individual who will require constant care and possibly cost state and/or federal taxpayer's money to support.

The pressure to abort is very real. Many believe that it's more merciful to prevent a child with disabilities from being born than to bring it into a life of suffering. Abortion, in their thinking, shows compassion to the child, to the parents, and to society by sparing it a burdensome expense. Also, the fear of facing a future without support from those closest to us is, I believe, a main factor for women who make this decision. Many in the Christian community energetically condemn women who have chosen abortion, but where is their energetic help for those who decide to keep the baby who needs extra care?

We do need to consider, though, the impact of those decisions to abort because of the likelihood of disability. If abortion is "the best decision," what does that say about choosing to give birth to a child with special needs? We may wonder, "If your child wasn't good enough to live, do you think mine is?" These types of questions have compelled the National Down Syndrome Congress to issue position statements to combat the current eugenics movement.

Among those positions are the call for legislation to guarantee the right to continue a pregnancy after prenatal diagnosis of Down syndrome and the right to refuse prenatal testing without repercussions from the medical community and insurance companies. The Congress also urges that people be educated about Down syndrome to ensure that raising such a child is not an insurmountable task for families to bear. If society can, in general, offer more help to support parents when they are faced with the possibility of raising a child with Down syndrome, the Congress hopes that abortion will not seem like the only option to them.

As part of their effort to educate the medical community, the Congress proposes that all medical students and practicing physicians be required to take a course in the political and social issues pertaining to disability. They also suggest that genetic counselors participate in an activity that lets them see an individual with a disability in a non-medical setting.

The Congress's most telling statement to a society so influenced by eugenic philosophy is a prohibition of wrongful life lawsuits. Parents could sue doctors for allowing their child with disabilities to live!

From the quest for perfection—it's a very small step to the intolerance for imperfection.

Euthanasia: Eliminating Imperfection

Euthanasia, also called mercy killing, is the "practice of ending a life so as to release an individual from an incurable disease or intolerable suffering."[12] Assisted suicide, which has gained notoriety through the efforts of Dr. Jack Kervorkian, is a form of euthanasia. Here a person may or may not be near death but feels that life has become unbearable and, in his or her mind, not worth living due to disease or disability. This form of euthanasia acts to deliberately cause the death of another; in contrast, a living will acts to not prolong the dying process by letting nature take its course.

Both of these forms are voluntary, but as history has shown us, the possibility of involuntary euthanasia is a very real and terrifying risk. Again we return to Nazi Germany, where eugenics and euthanasia went hand in hand.

In *Victims of the Nazis: 1933—1945*, we learn that "forced sterilization in Germany was the forerunner of the systematic killing of the mentally ill and the handicapped.

> In October 1939, Hitler himself initialed a decree
> which empowered physicians to grant a "mercy death"
> to "patients considered incurable according to the best
> available human judgment of their state of health."
> The intent of the so-called "euthanasia"program,
> however, was not to relieve the suffering of the
> chronically ill. . . . Its aim was to exterminate the
> mentally ill and the handicapped, thus "cleansing"the
> Aryan race of persons considered genetically defective
> and a financial burden to society.[13]

A book written in the 1920s, paved the way for this philosophy. In it, psychiatrist Alfred Hoche and criminal law scholar Karl Binding, "argued that economic savings justified the killing of 'useless lives' ('idiots' and 'congenitally crippled')"[14]

Where the Nazi regime publicly promoted its program of eugenics, it kept secret its plan of euthanasia. The Nazis even gave it a code name: Operation T4, an abbreviation of the headquarters' address, Tiergartenstrasse 4. A personal physician of Hitler's headed up the program, which involved sending questionnaires to all nursing homes and sanitariums regarding each patient's health and ability to work. Regarding children,

> doctors and other medical officials drew up
> detailed criteria for children who were to be "referred
> for treatment" under the new policy. Diseases which
> had to be referred included "idiocy and mongolism...
> deformities of every kind, in particular the absence of
> limbs, spina bifida, etc." Forms were returned to a
> Reich committee, from whence they were sent to three
> pediatricians who acted as assessors. They marked
> each form with a plus sign if the child were to die, or a
> minus sign if the child were to survive. None of the
> three doctors who made the judgment saw any of the
> children: they decided on the information of the forms
> alone.[15]

Adults also received a red plus sign of death or a blue minus sign of life, and occasionally a question mark for cases that needed further assessment. As with the children, the fate of adults with disabilities was decided from the questionnaire alone. What happened to those who received the red plus sign?

> *The doomed were bused to [six] killing centers in Germany and Austria—walled-in fortresses, mostly former psychiatric hospitals, castles and a former prison. . . . In the beginning, patients were killed by lethal injection. But by 1940,Hitler, on the advice of Dr. Werner Heyde [a psychiatrist and consultant to the Gestapo], suggested that carbon monoxide gas be used as the preferred method of killing.*[16]

This technique for mass murder would later be transferred to concentration camps, as would the crematoriums used to dispose of the bodies of the disabled. Between January 1940 and August 1941, 70,273 people had died by gassing at the six euthanasia centers. Although Hitler ordered Operation T4 stopped in August 1941, he encouraged physicians to continue using euthanasia to rid the Reich of people he deemed "useless eaters" and "life unworthy of life." When it was all over, as many as 250,000 people with mental or physical disabilities had been murdered between 1939 and 1945.

This is what happened when a society stopped valuing every person's life. Some were deemed more worthy of living than others. Human life became less precious than money. People took it into their own hands to "fix" the human race according to the design of their own prejudices.[17]

We cannot afford to think that it could never happen again. Every time our society looks to genetics to create perfection and to death as an answer to the pain of imperfection, we become less human—-because we've diminished our capacity to empathize and care—to reach out to others with compassion and love.

Abuse: Punishing the Imperfect

We in America haven't yet reached the horrible climax of the Nazi regime, but many in our culture have lost their compassion and care—even those who are supposed to be caregivers.

Consider the dilemma of parents who must face the possibility of out-of-home placement for their child with disabilities. Barb and Dave, whose son Brad has multiple disabilities—autism, legally blind, and nonverbal—is normally a sweet-spirited boy. Recently, however, he has shown regressive tendencies. Barb and Dave contacted a neurologist, who, after ruling out a brain tumor through an MRI, bluntly told them that their son's behavior was simply due to the fact that he was maturing, that he would soon become aggressive, and that he would need to be "institutionalized."

To say the least, Barb and Dave were stunned. She reflected:

> Out-of-home placement has crossed our minds many, many times. And I guess we view it as something that we take one day at a time. We will keep Brad at home as long as we can, without it becoming so overwhelming that the rest of the family is completely torn apart.
>
> I must admit, I have a high level of anxiety if I spend time thinking about it, simply because of my background. . . . When I worked as a caseworker at the state's disability center, I saw case after case of abuse. These were elementary-aged children and young adults. The care facilities often hire workers who are unfamiliar with caring for those with disabilities. There were all kinds of abuse, often perpetrated on those who were nonverbal.
>
> Dave and I almost feel as though we're bargaining with God; we know He will provide, but if it turns out that Brad has more issues above and beyond the obvious, we do hope that we will outlive him.

Although many long-term care institutions have excellent track records, there is an unfortunate reality of abuse that we parents cannot ignore when considering this option for our children. While we will work to do the best we can for our children, unfortunately there are those who view patients' limitations as a green light to mistreat them. This is a serious reality that we cannot ignore when faced with the difficult decision of long-term care. Fortunately, we can bring all our concerns to God in prayer, as He knows what is best for our little ones.

What the World Misses

It often seems like the world would like to eliminate all the physical and social imperfections it sees by attempting to create a society after its idea of perfection. But even as it makes its decisions, it's guided by prejudice, fear, intolerance, greed, hatred, and imperfect knowledge. These are the things that pollute and corrupt the human race, not physical or mental disabilities!

What the world needs is the redemption and renewal that only God can bring: "If anyone is in Christ, he is a new creation; the old has gone, the new has come! All this is from God, who reconciled us to himself through Christ"(2 Cor. 5:17—18). To those who discover their long-denied poverty, blindness, and nakedness, Christ counsels them as He does His own church:

> *"Buy from me gold refined in the fire, so you can become rich; and white clothes to wear, so you can cover your shameful nakedness; and salve to put on your eyes, so you can see.*
> *"... Here I am! I stand at the door and knock. If anyone hears my voice and opens the door, I will come in and eat with him, and he with me." (Rev. 3:18—20)*

The world needs to be re-created in the image of the only perfect Person who ever lived: Jesus Christ. Jesus is the "exact representation" of God's being, the One who sums up the Lord's heart and plan for His people. Bringing others to Him, as we'll explore in our next chapter, is part of the work we have to do.

CHAPTER 11

We Have Work to Do (Part 2)

For we are God's workmanship,
created in Christ Jesus
to do good works, which God
prepared in advance for us to do.
(EPH. 2:10)

After trekking through the harsh, intolerant wasteland of eugenics, euthanasia, and abuse, we need the refreshment of a cool, green oasis! Thankfully, we have such a place to go to in the Lord's loving, gentle heart. Through Him, we'll find the humility to accept human imperfection in ourselves and in others. In Him, we'll see the compassion He lavishes on us all— regardless of our giftedness or limitations, our abilities or disabilities. And with Him, we'll learn how to model and communicate His heart of compassionate love to our children, our families, our churches, and our communities.

God values every living being He has created—He is the author of each of our stories! This isn't just wishful or sentimental thinking; it's the truth which He has given to us through His Word. So let's trace His thoughts in Scripture. This will provide us with a firm foundation for understanding the work He has called us to do.

The Heart of God

Where the world often makes no place for children with disabilities (or for the Lord who made them, for that matter), God cherishes their presence and welcomes them eagerly—even if they cannot see, hear, speak, or move—even if their bodies are twisted or missing limbs. Do you remember Jesus' words to the Pharisees?

> *"When you give a luncheon or dinner, do not invite your friends, your brothers or relatives, or your rich neighbors; if you do, they may invite you back and so you will be repaid. But when you give a banquet, invite the poor, the crippled, the lame, the blind, and you will be blessed. Although they cannot repay you, you will be repaid at the resurrection of the righteous." (Luke 14:12—14)*

We human beings constantly base a person's value and desirability on his or her looks, status, wealth, or accomplishments, don't we? But clearly God does not. He welcomes everyone to His kingdom banquet (see vv. 16—21). And He wants us, the people called by His name, to be a welcoming community as well. He wants us to acknowledge and affirm the sacredness of human life, because He fashioned it in His own sacred image.

God Bestowed His Own Image on Us

Our children with disabilities have purpose and value because they, like every other person on this planet, have been created by God in His own image. The first chapter of Genesis tells us:

> *God created man in his own image,*
> *in the image of God he created him;*
> *male and female he created them. (v. 27)*

Not only are we made in God's own image, but the Lord personally fashions each of us in the womb, as David writes in Psalm 139:

For you created my inmost being;
you knit me together in my mother's womb. . . .
My frame was not hidden from you
when I was made in the secret place.
When I was woven together in the depths of the earth,
your eyes saw my unformed body.
All the days ordained for me
were written in your book
before one of them came to be. (vv. 13, 15—16)

Amazingly, the Lord's creative work in our lives takes place even before we're conceived, as He told Jeremiah:

"Before I formed you in the womb I knew you,
before you were born I set you apart;
I appointed you as a prophet to the nations." (Jer. 1:5)

Back in the creation narrative, we see God exulting in everything He made, because it was "good" (Gen. 1:3, 10, 12, 18, 21, 25). At the end of the sixth day, Scripture tells us that "God saw all that he had made, and it was very good" (v. 31, emphasis added).

Do you know what this means? God doesn't look at our children and say, "Oops" or "Yuck, that one didn't turn out right." Even their disabilities are in the Lord's hands, as He told Moses:

"Who gave man his mouth? Who makes him deaf or
mute? Who gives him sight or makes him blind? Is it not
I, the Lord?" (Exod. 4:11)

Our children with special needs are still the Lord's creation and are still very good. If they are neurologically, physically, or genetically impaired, they nevertheless remain complex and wonderful beings, "fearfully and wonderfully made" (Ps. 139:14). They are as intricately designed as anyone else is and fulfill God's purpose of reflecting His image in their lives.

What does it mean to be made in God's image? Because God is spirit, we know that His image can't be limited to our bodies. No, we find our likeness to the Lord in our inner qualities. Once we understand this, it may be easier to see how our children—whether their disabilities are mild or severe—still reflect some facet of God. Perhaps it's in their humility or gentleness. Maybe it comes out in their exuberance or affection. You might see something of the Lord in their patience or kindness or long-suffering.

Something in our children, no matter how uniquely they are challenged, speaks of God and His character. He made us that way...all of us. And because He, as our sovereign Creator, values each one of us, we need to recognize and stand firm in the intrinsic value of each other—especially of our children with disabilities. They are not mistakes, accidents, or punishments but the apple of God's eye—true gifts fashioned by the Lord's creative, compassionate hands.

God Is Compassionate

The dictionary defines compassion as a "sympathetic consciousness of others' distress together with a desire to alleviate it."[1]   God defines Himself by this quality:

[The Lord] passed in front of Moses, proclaiming, "The LORD, the LORD, the compassionate and gracious God, slow to anger, abounding in love and faithfulness."[2] (Exod. 34:6)

"For the LORD your God is a compassionate God." (Deut. 4:31a NASB)

He will have compassion on the poor and needy, And the lives of the needy he will save. (Ps. 72:13 NASB)

Praise the LORD, O my soul, and forget not all his benefits . . . who redeems your life from the pit and crowns you with love and compassion. (Ps. 103:2a, 4)

The LORD is gracious and righteous;
our God is full of compassion.
The LORD protects the simplehearted;
when I was in great need, he saved me. (Ps. 116:5—6)

Yet the LORD longs to be gracious to you;
he rises to show you compassion.
For the LORD is a God of justice.
Blessed are all who wait for him! (Isa. 30:18)

> *But when Jesus heard this, He said, "It is not those*
> *who are healthy who need a physician, but those who*
> *are sick. But go and learn what this means: 'I desire*
> *compassion, and not sacrifice,' for I did not come to*
> *call the righteous but sinners." (Matt. 9:12—13 NASB)*
>
> *When [Jesus] saw the crowds, he had compassion*
> *on them, because they were harassed and helpless,*
> *like sheep without a shepherd. (Matt. 9:36)*

Our Lord rules and responds to His world with heartfelt compassion and mercy. He doesn't turn away in disgust from broken lives and broken bodies. Rather, He reaches out and touches those we've labeled untouchable. He doesn't look with contempt at human need; instead, His heart is deeply moved by the pain and confusion He sees. And He doesn't abandon or devalue those who can't "contribute to society," but He seeks to welcome and protect the weak, needy, and vulnerable.

God Works through and Cares for the Vulnerable

In God's system of values, human strength doesn't count as much as openness to His power and grace. Paul told us in 1 Corinthians:

> *Brothers, think of what you were when you were called.*
> *Not many of you were wise by human standards; not*
> *many were influential; not many were of noble birth.*
> *But God chose the foolish things of the world to shame*
> *the wise; God chose the weak things of the world to*

shame the strong. He chose the lowly things of this world and the despised things—and the things that are not—to nullify the things that are, so that no one may boast before him. It is because of him that you are in Christ Jesus, who has become for us wisdom from God—that is, our righteousness, holiness and redemption. Therefore, as it is written: "Let him who boasts boast in the Lord." (1:26—31; see also Jer. 9:23—24)

God asks us to take our eyes off ourselves and direct the weak and the lowly toward the One who delights to make us righteous, holy, and redeemed!

Think of how the Lord has worked through human weakness. Through Abraham and Sarah, an elderly and childless couple, He created an entire nation of people. Through Moses, a former prince turned fugitive, He freed His people. Through David, the nearly forgotten son in a large family, He fashioned a dynasty through which the Messiah would come. And through Mary, a young, unmarried virgin, He brought the Savior of the world.

And what could be weaker than a newborn infant, humbler than a baby born in an animals' stall? Yet this is how God's own Son came to us—not in the power of wealth but in the helplessness of poverty. What could be weaker than being outnumbered, beaten, nailed naked to a cross, and placed in a borrowed tomb? Yet that is how the Lord conquered sin and death for us and brought us salvation!

As the Lord tells us:

"'Not by might nor by power, but by my Spirit,' says the Lord Almighty." (Zech. 4:6)

Not only does God use our weakness as a window to His power, but He commands that we protect those who are weak and vulnerable in society. Taste a few samples from His smorgasbord of care:

Righteousness and justice are the foundation of your throne;
love and faithfulness go before you. (Ps. 89:14; see also Deut. 32:4)

He who oppresses the poor shows contempt for their
Maker,
but whoever is kind to the needy honors God. (Prov.
14:31)

"Speak up for those who cannot speak for themselves,
for the rights of all who are destitute.
Speak up and judge fairly;
defend the rights of the poor and needy."
(Prov. 31:8—9)

"He defended the cause of the poor and needy,
and so all went well.
Is that not what it means to know me?"
declares the LORD. (Jer. 22:16; see also Deut. 24:17)

"'I myself will tend my sheep and have them lie down,
declares the Sovereign LORD. I will search for the lost
and bring back the strays. I will bind up the injured and
strengthen the weak.'" (Ezek. 34:15—16a)

And the word of the LORD came again to Zechariah:
"This is what the Lord Almighty says: 'Administer true
justice; show mercy and compassion to one another.
Do not oppress the widow or the fatherless, the alien or
the poor. In your hearts do not think evil of each
other.'" (Zech. 7:8—10; see also Isa. 1:17; Mic. 6:8)

"Woe to you Pharisees, because you give God a tenth
of your mint, rue and all other kinds of garden herbs,
but you neglect justice and the love of God." (Luke
11:42a)

"By this kind of hard work we must help the weak,
remembering the words the Lord Jesus himself said: 'It is
more blessed to give than to receive.'" (Acts 20:35)

And we urge you, brothers, warn those who are idle, encourage the timid, help the weak, be patient with everyone. (1 Thess. 5:14)

The world may see no value or use in children who aren't smart or strong or beautiful, but that's because its values are upside down and backwards! The Lord of the universe, the Creator of all, wants everyone who is vulnerable to be protected, included, and embraced. He wants justice guaranteed for them, kindness and care readily extended to them, and respect gladly shown to them.

And because we're His people, He wants us to do the same.

Our Work: Reflecting God's Heart through the Prism of Disabilities

How do we reveal God's heart for special children to a world that doesn't often see their value? Do we need to embark on a Don Quixote-like crusade to right the world's wrongs? Perhaps some are called to that, but knowing myself, I'd probably get tangled up in a windmill!

I think we can reflect God's values in some very practical ways, including (1) the often unseen care we provide for our children day after day, (2) educating ourselves and others about our children's condition and needs, and (3) advocating for them in church, at school, and in society when their needs are being ignored and their dignity trampled.

Our Daily Care

Let's face it, families with children who have special needs do more work. We have to contend with more paperwork, we talk with more doctors and insurance companies, and we argue with more teachers than the average parent. And this is on top of all the regular stuff of life: paying bills, doing laundry, dealing with coworkers, etc.

It would be easy to become overwhelmed, because sometimes the tasks are overwhelming. But if in our fatigue we can still take care of our children lovingly, then we have served the Lord and championed His values.

For example, when we patiently change the diaper on a wiggling twelve-year-old, we reflect the Lord's patience. When we diligently clean our infant's gastronomy tube, we reflect the Lord's faithful care. When we tenderly and consistently care for a child who never responds, we reflect the Lord's unconditional love. And when we endure the nasty looks and comments of others as our child tantrums in public without glaring back, we reflect the Lord's grace.

Many people will never see the medications we administer or the therapies we apply. I'm convinced that nobody really sees all the work that goes into caring for our children, because a lot of that work is emotional. But God sees it all. And when people see us in a public setting caring for our children with patience and love, our actions speak volumes about the power of Christ, who enables us to do these things day in and day out.

Who knows, we might even spur someone on to reflect on what our world could (and should) be. Theologian Stanley Hauerwas presents a perspective that people probably don't often think about:

> The issue is not whether [children with special needs] can serve a human good, but whether we should be the kind of people, the kind of parents and community, that can receive, even welcome, them into our midst in a manner that allows them to flourish.[3]

Our faithful care shows others what life is like when we become the kind of people who welcome children with disabilities and help them flourish! Don't underestimate the power of your love for your child. As Paul encouraged us, "Let us not become weary in doing good, for at the proper time we will reap a harvest if we do not give up" (Gal. 6:9).

Educating Ourselves and Others

The next way we can reflect God's heart and values to the world begins with educating ourselves about the Lord and the special child He has given us. We especially need to understand how central compassion is to the way of Christ. Then we will be able to help our churches grasp this so we can, together, take God's message to the world.

Teaching Ourselves

If we want others to understand what our children are about, we need to be good students of our kids first. Part of our work as parents is to learn about our children—what their strengths and weaknesses are, what method of training is most effective and constructive, what upsets them, what scares them, what makes them happy.

Having a solid understanding of their disabilities is obviously essential too. We can take the edge off of some of our frustrations when we understand why our child balks at certain things. What at first glance looks like willful disobedience may really be a neurological reaction to certain stimuli. Having this knowledge and insight will help us better interact with, train, and instruct our child in the way he or she should go (see Prov. 22:6).

I would encourage you to take advantage of the wealth of resources available to parents with differently-abled children today. You can probably find a plethora of books and magazines at your local library. Also, many school districts can put you in touch with parent advocacy groups connected with a variety of disorders. And no matter how rare your child's disability, a support group has probably been formed for it that offers a newsletter you can subscribe to. Last but not least, the internet holds a cornucopia of information on almost every disability that exists. It offers websites devoted to specific disabilities, parent-to-parent support and networking groups, seminars, clearinghouses for pamphlets and books, as well as legal resources and policies related to disabilities.

One warning, though: if your child has a well-known disability, such as Down's syndrome, cerebral palsy, or autism, watch out for the avalanche of information. Wade through it carefully, choose the information that makes sense for you and your child, and discard the rest. And where the internet is concerned, it may be helpful to set a time limit for yourself, because you could spend days staring at the screen, numbing your neurons in the process!

Since we're also concerned with reflecting God's heart regarding our special child, we would do well to spend a lot of thoughtful time in Scripture and in prayer. With a concordance in your lap, look up what God has to say about those with disabilities through such words as "blind," "deaf," "lame," and "mute." Or trace out different themes that reveal the Lord's nature, such as His mercy, kindness, justice, and compassion. We've already looked at God's compassion, but did you know that Jesus commands us to be compassionate too? "Be compassionate as your Father is compassionate," He said in Luke's gospel (Luke 6:36 NEB). And Paul echoed Christ's teaching:

> *Therefore, as God's chosen people, holy and dearly loved, clothe yourselves with compassion, kindness, humility, gentleness and patience. (Col. 3:12)*

Teaching Others

Part of our call to educate involves teaching others about God's worldview; and compassion——not physical and mental perfection——is at the heart of that. In their book <u>Compassion: A Reflection on the Christian Life</u>, Henri Nouwen, Donald McNeill, and Douglas Morrison explain that Jesus' command to be compassionate

> *...is a command to participate in the compassion of God himself. He requires us to unmask the illusion of our competitive selfhood, to give up clinging to our imaginary distinctions as sources of identity, and to be taken up into the same intimacy with God which [Jesus] himself knows. This is the mystery of the Christian life: to receive a new self, a new identity, which depends not on what we can achieve, but on what we are willing to receive. . . .*
> *This new self, the self of Jesus Christ, makes it possible for us to be compassionate as our Father is compassionate.[4]*

Perhaps you could start a Bible study or work with your church's Bible study leader to teach others about how God's values relate to people with disabilities. Or maybe you could invite your pastor to attend one of your parent support group meetings so he could get a better understanding of what your lives are like and how the church can better respond.

Churches, believe it or not, often need more educating than the world. More than once I have heard parents of special children say they were asked to leave a church because there was "no place for them" there. How tragic. Where public schools have been mandated to provide an appropriate education for all students, churches often deny a child with disabilities appropriate spiritual education. Where federal law (through the Americans with Disabilities Act) now requires public buildings and spaces to accommodate people with disabilities—through such means as extra wide and close parking places, wheelchair ramps, and special restroom stalls, for example—churches remain exempt. So if your church has wheelchair access and special parking, you are seeing the heart of your church.

I'm going to make a bold statement: a church that fails to welcome and serve all who wish to attend, especially those with disabilities, disobeys Christ's commands to "love your neighbor as yourself" and "be compassionate as your Father is compassionate." In the <u>Pastoral Statement of U.S. Catholic Bishops on People with Disabilities</u>, the bishops provide all Christians with these insights:

> The central meaning of Jesus' ministry is bound up with the fact that He sought the company of people who, for one reason or another, were forced to live on the fringe of society. (cf. Mk. 7:37) These He made the special object of His attention, declaring that the last would be first and that the humble would be exalted in His Father's kingdom. (cf. Mt. 20:16, 23:12) The Church finds its true identity when it fully integrates itself with these marginal people, including those who suffer from physical and psychological disabilities.
>
> If people with disabilities are to become equal partners in the Christian community, injustices must be eliminated and ignorance and apathy replaced by increased sensitivity and warm acceptance. The leaders and the general membership of the Church must educate themselves to appreciate fully the

contribution people with disabilities can make to the Church's spiritual life. They bring with them a special insight into the meaning of life; for they live, more than the rest of us perhaps, in the shadow of the cross. And out of their experience they forge virtues like courage, patience, perseverance, compassion and sensitivity that should serve as an inspiration to all Christians.[5]

How can we help our churches include those who are so easily excluded?

• *Pray.* Pray about who to meet with—probably the head pastor or someone else on the church staff who might have his ear. Pray about when to meet with this person, preferably not around Christmas or Easter. And also pray about whether you should meet with someone at all. Perhaps God is calling you to a different place of worship that's more welcoming to your child.

• *Be prepared.* Know precisely how you would like to see your child included. Then offer some concrete ideas about how to accomplish this. You might also want to give your pastor or church staff a disability awareness package to help in your cause. (See the recommended resources at the end of this book.)

• *Be gracious.* Making a way for our children when there doesn't appear to be one can stir up strong emotions and frustration. Rather than issuing angry demands, pretend it's you who knows nothing about disability and educate accordingly.

• *Be patient.* Starting any new program takes time and often involves lots of error. Make sure you're staying in prayer, and if it looks like your cause is going nowhere, ask God for wisdom about how to proceed. He's only too happy to let you know which direction you should go in next, and He can lead you to other individuals who will help you.

Our children's schoolteachers may also need to be educated about our children's disabilities, and about who our kids are apart from their special needs. It's so easy for teachers to label and categorize children, so we need to keep our children's individuality at the forefront.

Often, teachers have received scant training regarding children with disabilities because special education is treated as a completely different credentialing program. So they may not know how to balance our child's needs with the needs of the rest of the class. As we seek to help the teacher understand our child's situation, we also need to seek to understand the teacher's situation. We can accomplish a lot more in an atmosphere of mutual understanding and respect.

Advocating for Our Children

Unfortunately, our fallen world guarantees that advocating for our children will at some point be a necessary part of our lives. Being an advocate means having to plead our child's cause—either speaking up for their rights or writing to someone to secure their rights. It often involves conflict, so we need to be careful about how to proceed in a way that honors God.

Before we go bursting into our local school district office or church, we need to know exactly what we want for our children and why. We also need to be sensitive to timing so that we don't win a battle that costs us the war. When is it proper to speak or more prudent to remain silent? A lot of times, the situation will clearly show us what we need to do. I would recommend always advocating in the following cases:

1. When we suspect that our children are being physically or verbally abused. Sometimes this can be harder to discern than we would assume, especially if our child is nonverbal. So we need to look for signs such as marks on the body or a change in behavior (more irritability, tantrums, or withdrawal). We should pay special attention to our children's resistive behavior when we drop them off at school, at a day program, or with a caretaker.

2. When we suspect that our children's needs, both physical and educational, are being ignored. If our children are regressing or stagnating rather than progressing, their teachers might have shuttled them to the back of the classroom and left

them there. If you have an inkling that this is happening, talk with the teacher or therapist, or drop in unscheduled sometime (a good program will permit this).

3. When we suspect that our children are being shut out of activities because "there is no place for them." Dealing with this kind of situation takes discernment, because we risk alienating people by forcing our children into situations they may not be able to handle or into the face of some people who will never welcome our child—-no matter what we do.

A Final Thought

Our children with special needs may look and sound less refined than typical children. They may dismay others with their loud noises, flailing arms, or drooling. And to be honest, aren't we ourselves sometimes put off by those who look or smell different? But the apostle James writes to all of us:

> Listen, dear friends. Isn't it clear by now that God operates quite differently? He chose the world's down-and-out as the kingdom's first citizens, with full rights and privileges. This kingdom is promised to anyone who loves God. And here you are abusing these same citizens! . . .
> Talk and act like a person expecting to be judged by the Rule that sets us free. For if you refuse to act kindly, you can hardly expect to be treated kindly. Kind mercy wins over harsh judgment every time. (James 2:5—6a, 12—13 THE MESSAGE)[6]

We need to ask ourselves if we are the kind of people who show respect to all people, regardless of appearance or status. As parents of children with special needs, it's easy to get upset when we feel someone has discriminated against us or our child. But life isn't a one-way street. We need to see if we do the same thing to someone with whom we feel uncomfortable.

Our platform for reform will be much more solid and firm if we can, with God's help, treat each person we meet with dignity and respect. Not just those who agree with us or treat us kindly, but even those who, despite all our educating and advocating, never care about our children's needs. To them we simply extend grace and leave them to God, who understands us and our children completely.

CHAPTER 12

Putting It into Perspective

We also rejoice in our sufferings,
because we know that
suffering produces perseverance;
perseverance, character;
and character, hope. And hope
does not disappoint us.
(ROM. 5:3—5A)

S ometimes I wonder what my life would have been like if my sons had not had special needs. Would it have seemed easier? Would I have doubted my parenting skills as much? Would the rough edges of my life have been illuminated as much as they have been by my special sons?

I know that raising a normal child is full of unforeseen challenges, too. From the outside looking in, it seems a lot easier, but I don't want to idealize it.

Because God had a different road for me, I may never know the answers to my questions. One thing I do know: I might never have been forced to face and acknowledge publicly my own shortcomings as a parent and as a human being. Also, I probably would never have met the fabulous people I know in the community of disability. I might never have known the depth of love our friends and family have for us. I would not have had the privilege of being able to help others who walk the same path that I do. And I might not have been impacted as deeply as I have by Christ's sufferings and the relationship He desires for us.

It may seem strange to some, but having a child with disabilities has many unique blessings and benefits—and I wouldn't trade my life for anyone else's if I could.

The Blessings of Raising a Child with Disabilities

Sometimes it's so easy to get caught up with all the medications, doctor visits, therapies, and hassles with insurance and school that we lose sight of the big picture. We lose sight of what God is trying to do in our lives. So let's step outside the maelstrom of our swirling activities and emotions and let the dust settle a bit. Let's get some perspective on some of the good that God is working together in our lives.

Burning Off the Dross

As I look back at my life, all of my early spiritual training now seems like "book work"—parenting children with disabilities has tested out my knowledge in the lab. And like any person who reads the book and then tries to actually perform the task, I discovered big gaps.

God knew I needed to be introduced to disability. He knew I needed to purge the meaningless dross from my life. I used to worry so much about maintaining an immaculate house, looking like the perfect family, fulfilling everyone else's expectations. If everything was perfect, then I was in control. If I was perfect, then God would love me.

Through my sons' disabilities, God drove those enslaving ideas out of my life like Christ drove the moneychangers out of the temple! He freed me from the tyranny of perfection. And He went on to do more.

Through my children's special needs, God helped me face my own weaknesses. He showed me my pride, which had deep roots in the center of my being and entangled all my ideas and attitudes. He showed me how much I needed a Savior. And I have learned that it is He alone who performs great miracles for my children.

It's not easy or pleasant for God to burn away the dross from our lives. Our emotional skin feels pink and tender, and our minds reel at what we see as if we had mental vertigo. But God doesn't keep us in the fire indefinitely. He watches for us to start taking the form He wants, and then He levels our mental horizon and dabs His balm on our emotional hurts.

There's nothing like the precious outcome—humility, peace, realness, and rest in God's grace. Knowing that the Lord wants our best will help us endure the process of getting there.

Admitting Need

I don't know about you, but I have trouble asking for help. I believe that God put me in a position of great weakness and confusion to force me to rely on His kindness through His servants and others. If you have been in a position of great physical, material, or spiritual need, you know the humiliation involved in asking others for help. To make your need known before God is one thing, but to make it known before others is another. However, if I had never made my need known before others, I could not have been comforted as I have been.

It took many months before I could admit to others that I was struggling with the diagnosis of autism for our second child. I didn't want to be seen as a whiner, a big drag, or someone in constant need of care. But one Sunday morning my desire to be strong cracked, and I tearfully asked for prayer in coping with our new future. Though it was hard for me, it brought about one of the best things that has ever happened in my life.

The leader of women's ministries, Robin, rallied several others around me and my friend Shelia, whose daughter Hayley had recently been diagnosed with leukemia. Robin wrote and distributed a wonderful letter that spurred many to send cards, letters, books, and other treats. I have saved every card and note and put them into a scrapbook. And for weeks I carried the letter in my pocket as a reminder of God's love through others. I'd like to share some of this letter with you:

> *Dear Friends,*
> *Within our New Community class at church there*
> *are two women who are currently carrying heavy*

burdens. They are dealing with the day-to-day reality of children who need a great deal of care, attention, and every bit of mothering they can give. . . . These ladies also have other children and their husbands who depend on them as well. We all know the nurturing role of woman/wife/mother is a gift from our good Lord, but it is not always easy. . . .

. . . I would like to suggest we come alongside these ladies in an unofficial but structured way in the next few months. What I have in mind is a "one week at a time, not so secret pal" type plan. If one of us each took Shelia and Michelle for a week at a time and devoted some TLC and committed prayer to them, we could insure they receive some extra support to ease their burden. . . .

Suggestions of ways to uplift these sisters—
• Letter with a tea bag or ice cream coupons

• Handpicked garden flowers

• A tea/coffee cup filled with a special treat

• Clip a cartoon and mail it

• A coupon offering a service

• Treats they would enjoy

• Deliver a devotional gift book to their doorstep

• Bubble bath or a new lipstick

• Your time!!! Make an appointment to let them talk about their child's care . . .

• A postcard every day that week

• Do a chore or errand for them

• Tell them they are doing a good job

- *Baby-sit for a date night*

- *Make a meal for them*

- *Hug them*

- *Mother the mother, treat them like the child we all sometimes wish we still were*

- *Pray for them and with them*

Just knowing that others were praying for us meant so much. In fact, just the letter itself was a source of great comfort. I pulled it out and looked at it often to remind myself that the Lord indeed did care about my sadness.

Throughout the following weeks, I received postcards, notes, and some books. One sweet friend, Cindy, came by with a casserole one evening. "I just didn't know what to do, so I made a casserole!" she said, almost apologetically. What a blessing it was. Since I didn't have the energy to fix meals, a home-cooked meal was most welcome. But it wasn't so much the food as it was the spirit in which it was given. Cindy wanted to help, so she did what she did best—prepared a meal. By profession, Cindy is a banquet planner, so meal planning is her gift. Each woman who took the time to encourage us was using the gifts God had given them.

My reason for including this letter is to encourage you to make your needs known to others. For some of us, asking for help or prayer doesn't come naturally. It's our personality to try to take care of things ourselves. Sometimes, if we're a long way from the initial diagnosis, we may feel we have lost the right to ask others for help. But we haven't. God wants to comfort us every step of the way, and He does this most often through the interdependent members of His body. As Paul taught us:

> *Praise be to the God and Father of our Lord Jesus Christ, the Father of compassion and the God of all comfort, who comforts us in all our troubles, so that we can comfort those in any trouble with the comfort we ourselves have received from God. (2 Cor. 1:3—4)*

Valuing Eternity

Before I had children with special needs, my faith in the living Christ was, I later discovered, rather one-dimensional. I thought that a strong faith would help me through the hard times in life, which it certainly does. But as Paul observed, "If being a Christian is of value to us only now in this life, we are the most miserable of creatures" (1 Cor. 15:19 LB). I came to realize that I had not been living with an eternal view. Heaven, I thought, came at the end of the road for those who love God and accept Christ as Savior—kind of like the happy ending to a good story. Life here with Christ seemed separate from life there. It never occurred to me that the work we begin here is the work we will continue in heaven.

When I couldn't make my children be like all the other children, it was like I was handed a new pair of glasses that helped me see beyond the here and now. The here and now hurt . . . it didn't make sense . . . it was impossible for me to get comfortable with it. But having eternity in view helped me gain some perspective on what I was going through. As Joni Eareckson Tada notes, "Our pain and longings make sure we will never be content, but that's good: it is to our benefit that we do not grow comfortable in a world destined for decay."[1]

This world isn't the "be all and end all" that I used to think it was—and that I could not think it was after my sons were born. I really don't see how people who have no eternal hope can make it here.

Even we who are Christian may feel helpless because our child with a disability will never walk, talk, nor be well. We may feel no hope in raising a child who cannot be like others—or who may never actually grow up at all. But because of Christ, we are promised that one day our children will be whole and eternally happy. And that hope can keep us going!

As we trust the Lord for our children's future as well as our own, what we read in Scripture becomes more real to us. Gerald Sittser describes this process:

> We reach the point where we begin to search for a
> new life, one that depends less on circumstances and
> more on the depth of our souls. . . . It begins to dawn on
> us that reality may be more than we once thought it to

be. *We begin to perceive hints of the divine, and our longing grows. . . . In the coming to the end of ourselves, we have come to the beginning of our true and deepest selves. We have found the One whose love gives shape to our being.*[2]

What promise does heaven hold for us? One day everything that hampers us here will be gone. Our disintegrating bodies, our penchant for selfish concerns, the thorns in our flesh will be removed. The prophet Isaiah said,

Say to those with fearful hearts,
"Be strong, do not fear;
your God will come, . . .
he will come to save you."
Then will the eyes of the blind be opened,
and the ears of the deaf unstopped.
Then will the lame leap like a deer,
and the mute tongue shout for joy. (Isa. 35:4—6)

Your child with cerebral palsy will walk; your child with autism will stop injuring himself; your child with mental retardation will converse with eloquence; your child who relies on machines and medications to function will walk free of them all. It will happen!

It will happen because God is merciful and has reserved for those who trust in Him a place where "the ransomed of the Lord will return. . . . Everlasting joy will crown their heads. Gladness and joy will overtake them, and sorrow and sighing will flee away" (v. 10). If we can just hold tight until we get there, heaven will clarify what looks murky now. We will finally figure out who God really is and who we and our child are in Him. "Now we see but a poor reflection as in a mirror; then we shall see face to face. Now I know in part; then I shall know fully, even as I am fully known" (1 Cor. 13:12). Joni Eareckson Tada adds, "On earth you may think you fully blossomed, but heaven will reveal that you barely budded."[3]

"Budded on Earth . . . Blossoming in Heaven" were the words Jim and Cindi used in memory of their infant son, Evan. Through prenatal testing, they had learned that their son had Trisomy 9

Mosaic Syndrome—he had an extra ninth chromosome, which contributes greatly to deficiencies in physical and mental capabilities. When he was born, he weighed only three pounds, one ounce. His lungs, heart, kidneys, and liver appeared to be functioning, but he had a severe hearing loss in his right ear.

At four months, he looked only weeks old and weighed a mere six pounds. But he started smiling and cooing at his sisters, Caitlyn and Lauren, who always wanted to hold him and kiss him.

When Evan was six months old, doctors determined that he had a malrotation problem with his intestines, which would need to be corrected with major surgery. He had tubes and IVs everywhere—a ventilator, a G-tube placed in his stomach, and he had a three- to four-inch incision across his small abdomen. After about a month in the hospital, Evan got to go home.

A little over a year later, however, Evan went home to his heavenly Father. Though doctors didn't think he'd live a year, and though at twenty-one months he weighed only eleven pounds, his death came as a shock to Jim and Cindi.

Even more surprising was that Jim, a profoundly hurting father, decided to give one of Evan's eulogies. His words put Evan's life, and the lives of all children with disabilities, into such perspective that the Lord had to be speaking through him:

> *"I would like to say thank you very much from Cindi and me on a personal note for all of you being here today. We appreciate all of you joining us, standing by us in our time of sorrow and also celebrating with us a very special life.*
>
> *Many of you were such an important part of Evan's life, whether you realized it or not. People often would comment to us on what a wonderful job they felt we did, or how much they admired us, or many other wonderful words of encouragement that we took to heart.*
>
> *But we want each of you to know that you were all involved in this ministry that God bestowed upon us. It was through your prayers and your support, sometimes in ways that seemed small and other ways very large. It was that support and encouragement that has allowed*

us as a family to fulfill the ministry to Evan that God gave us. It freed us to serve Him.

I have thought over the last few days that I wanted to say something today to honor Evan, and I felt the best way to do that would be to share something from our unique perspective. Something that God has taught us and how He changed us through Evan.

The Lord put Cindi and me into a very unique situation in which we had no control. As much as we wanted to, we couldn't change anything about our son. We found ourselves in a very unique position, a precarious position emotionally, where our hearts were overflowing with requests for his condition. Our desires were for his healing, his growth, and his wholeness. Yet our minds kept asking us again and again, Is there really any hope for our little boy? Through all of that, God brought us to a better understanding of the balance between our supplication, pouring out our hearts and making our requests made known to him as the Bible tells us we ought to do, and yet surrendering those desires to the completeness of His sovereign will.

God taught us something about the depths of trust. Many of you shared with us how Evan's life, and in particular his innocence, has touched you, and we treasure that now as we remember God's unfailing faithfulness to us through many hard-learned lessons.

Most importantly, I think to truly honor Evan, and through that to honor God for His purpose in what He taught us all through Evan, we need to ask ourselves how God changed each of us through Evan's life. Please do not leave here today feeling that you are somehow on the outside of this experience looking in. Evan's life was not about our family or possibly a select few who were involved with him on a weekly basis. Evan's life is a challenge to each and every one of us to accept what God chooses for us each day. Far greater is the faith expressed in simply accepting God's will in any situation than simply somehow trying to claim our own outcomes or desires.

Pastor Curt has been with us from the beginning of our journey with Evan and he has shared a lot of things over the past few days with us. One of the things that he has showed us that really touched my heart, and even in these last few days has brought many things together for me, was this writing called "Two Minutes to Eternity." It was written by Marshall Shelley, who was a parent, a father who lost two little children at a very young age. The reason that I think it has become special to me is that it asks and addresses many of the questions that I struggled with early on and continued to throughout Evan's twenty-one months. Some of the questions of why.

I don't think it takes someone with a special child to ask these kinds of questions, but why would God create life to last such a short time? And why would He create a life that is so limited and so restrictive in our view? I would like to read part of this.

Shelley writes, "The apostle John's vision of eternity suggests what is in store for all the saints: 'The throne of God and of the Lamb will be in the city, and his servants will serve him. They will see his face, and his name will be on their foreheads. . . . And they will reign forever and ever' (Rev. 22:3—5).'"

Shelley goes on to say, "I don't know exactly how we will serve, nor can I be specific about how we will assist in reigning. But those tasks sound like they have more significance than most careers we pursue in our lifetimes. Could it be that when I finally start the most significant service of my life, I will find that this is what I was truly created for? I may find I was created not for what I would accomplish on earth, but for the role I would fulfill in heaven."

Why did God create a child to live for twenty-one months? He didn't. God created Evan for eternity. And He created each and every one of us for eternity, where we may be surprised to find our true calling, which always seemed just out of reach here on earth."

God, the Master Planner, laid out all these events—Evan's life, our special child's life—before the foundations of the earth were laid. His plans for us are what none of us would ever have expected. When they are completed in eternity, we will see that they, like our children, are a glorious and most unexpected gift.

Would You Remove Your Child's Disability If You Could?

Here's some food for thought: If you could eliminate your child's disability in this lifetime, would you do so? What would you gain and lose in the process? What are some of the reasons you would or wouldn't? How do they relate to your faith in God and your acceptance of His plan for your life, if at all?

Several parents I spoke to answered with an emphatic "Yes!" to this question. If Barb could, she would erase Brad's disabilities "in a heartbeat." Though her faith has been strengthened through Brad's life, she still looks forward to the day when her son "will someday be made whole, and we will spend eternity with him, talking and catching up on the years he was trapped in a body and unable to communicate."

Another special mom would eliminate her daughter's disability because of the heartache it causes her little girl. "If I could erase it for my daughter, I would in a minute, because I see how she struggles. I see how close she is to being like everybody else and yet so far away, and how much she wants to be there. So my heart aches for her. Yet, I think of all the opportunities that we have had as family, the people we have ministered to, and who have ministered to us. And in that regard, I feel very blessed to be in the situation that we are in. But for our daughter's sake, I would erase her disability if I could."

For other parents, the question of erasing a child's special needs is more complex. "I've thought about that," says Ruth, regarding her son. "Yes and no. I'm saying yes for the fact that it would give him a better chance going through life. And I have to admit yes would be for selfish reasons too—I have to be honest, it would make it easier to raise him. But I'd also say no because that would change who he is, and I don't want to change who he is. He has his own personality and his own uniqueness, and if I erased his special need that would take away that uniqueness."

And Claudia would definitely not eliminate her son's disability. "I have not tried praying for a cure," she says, because "my faith doesn't say that that's something I can ask for." Because God fashioned her son in the womb this way, Claudia says, "I don't feel like I can honestly pray for that. Maybe I've got too little faith, but that's where I am." I asked her if she would she bypass this journey if she could go back to the beginning, before the inception of her son's disability. "Well, theoretically and theologically, I would say no. I firmly believe that everything is in God's plan. And if He had wanted [our son] to be different, He would have made him different. I have to believe that God is working all things for good. . . . There are lots of things that could be different, but I think overall I will trust God that He's got the best."

All theoretical questions aside, the bottom line is that we couldn't love our kids any more than we already do. When my children were struggling more to make their needs known, it was hard sometimes to feel the rewards of parenting. But it never stopped me from loving them. In fact, I would have given my life for them should someone have tried to harm them. Nothing they could ever say or do could make me love them more.

And now that both my boys, despite their challenges, are growing up to be delightful, sometimes whimsical young men, I find that their newfound accomplishments don't make me feel more affection for them. Jim and I are proud, beyond proud actually, of how far they have come! They have exceeded expectations of most of the educators and medical professionals. Daniel's insight, sense of humor, incredible visual memory, and love of animals make him a delight. Jonathan's winsomeness and incredible thirst for knowledge are stunning.

In addition to the patience they show toward others, the love they have for each other and the way they treat each other most of the time is really amazing to me. They stick up for one another, they are mostly patient with each other, and they help each other out. They are nice boys, just the way God made them.

Think of how your children delight you—and what they teach us all. When we see our children's acceptance of those around them and their sweet grins, we are reminded of how we should treat others. When we see them working hard to accomplish what seems to be a small task in the world's eyes, we are reminded that God doesn't need us to perform many tasks for Him. He just expects us to perform the ones He has set in front of us. Our children are living reminders that our hearts and diligence matter more to God than all of our accomplishments.

As we raise and love our special children—our special gifts from God—let's take the Apostle Paul's words with us:

Throw yourselves into the work of the Master, confident that nothing you do for him is a waste of time or effort. . . .

Keep your eyes open, hold tight to your convictions, give it all you've got, be resolute, and love without stopping. (1 Cor. 15:58; 16:13—14 THE MESSAGE)[4]

✸✸✸

Never give up. Though our bodies are dying, our inner strength in the Lord is growing every day. These troubles and sufferings of ours are, after all, quite small and won't last very long. . . . So we do not look at what we can see right now, the troubles all around us, but we look forward to the joys in heaven which we have not yet seen. The troubles will soon be over, but the joys to come will last forever. (2 Cor. 4:16—18 LB)

Footnotes

Chapter Three
1. Lewis B. Smedes, *Forgive and Forget: Healing the Hurts We Don't Deserve* (New York: Pocket Books, 1984), p.179.
2. Joni Eareckson Tada and Steve Estes, *When God Weeps: Why Our Sufferings Matter to the Almighty* (Grand Rapids: Zondervan Publishing House, 1997), pp. 83, 85-86.
3. Smedes, *Forgive and Forget*, p.115.

Chapter Four
1. Gerald Sittser, *A Grace Disguised: How the Soul Grows Through Loss* (Grand Rapids: Zondervan Publishing House, 1996), p.56.
2. C. S. Lewis, *A Grief Observed* (New York: Bantam Books, 1961), pp.1, 3.
3. Cheri Fuller and Louise Tucker Jones, *Extraordinary Kids* (Colorado Springs, Colorado: Focus on the Family, 1997), p.174.

Chapter Five
1. Philip Yancey, *Disappointment with God* (Grand Rapids: Zondervan Publishing House, 1988), p. 207.

Chapter Six
1. Eugene H. Peterson, *The Message: The Wisdom Books* (Colorado Springs, Colorado: NavPress, 1996), p. 74.
2. Eugene H. Peterson, *The Message: The New Testament in Contemporary English* (Colorado Springs, Colorado: NavPress, 1993), p. 407.
3. Ronald Youngblood, note on Genesis 32:24, in *The NIV Study Bible*, 10th anniversary edition, gen. Ed. Kenneth L. Barker (Grand Rapids: Zondervan Publishing House, 1995), p. 55.

Chapter Seven
1. Eugene H. Peterson, *The Message: The New Testament in Contemporary English* (Colorado Springs, Colorado: NavPress, 1993), pp. 384-85.
2. Paul Barnett, *The Message of 2 Corinthians: Power in Weakness*, The Bible Speaks Today Series, (Downers Grove, Illinois: InterVarsity Press, 1988), pp. 179-80.
3. K. C. Cole, "One Thing is Perfectly Clear: Nothingness is Perfect," *The Los Angeles Times*, December 14, 2000, Section B2
4. Philip Yancey, *What's So Amazing About Grace?* (Grand Rapids: Zondervan Publishing House, 1997), p. 273.

Chapter Nine
1. Robert Frost, "The Road Not Taken," in *Robert Frost's Poems*, comp. Louis Untermeyer (New York: Pocket Books, 1971), p. 223
2. Paul Tournier, *Guilt and Grace*, trans. Arthur W. Heathcote, J. J. Henry, and P. J. Allcock (San Francisco: Harper and Row, 1962), pp. 98-99.

3. Tournier, *Guilt and Grace*, p. 95.
4. Eugene H. Peterson, *The Message: The New Testament in Contemporary English* (Colorado Springs, Colorado: NavPress, 1993), p. 21.
5. *Webster's New Word Dictionary of the American Language*, 2d College Ed., see "courage."
6. Tournier, quoting his wife, *Guilt and Grace*, p. 99.
7. C. S. Lewis, *The Business of Heaven: Daily Readings from C. S. Lewis*, ed. Walter Hooper (San Diego: Harcourt Brace Jovanovich, 1984), p. 18.
8. Frederick Buechner, *Wishful Thinking: A Seeker's ABC*, rev. and exp. Ed. (San Francisco: HarperSanFrancisco, 1993), p. 58.
9. Peterson, *The Message*, p. 399.

Chapter Ten

1. Robyn Dixon, "Adoption Brings Joy to One Family, Pain to Another, *Los Angeles Times*, February 18, 2001, section A, pp. 1, 12.
2. "Eugenics," *Microsoft Encarta 1994*. Microsoft (registered mark) Encarta. Copyright (copyright mark) 1993 Microsoft Corporation. Copyright (copyright mark) 1993 Funk & Wagnall's Corporation.
3. "Eugenics," *Microsoft Encarta 1994*.
4. Gina Maranto, *Quest for Perfection: The Drive to Breed Better Human Beings* (New York: Simon & Schuster, A Lisa Drew Book/Scribner, 1996) pp. 146-47.
5. As quoted by Arthur J. Dyck, "Eugenics in Historical and Ethical Perspective," in *Genetic Ethics: Do the Ends Justify the Genes?*, ed, John F. Kilner, Rebecca D. Pentz, and Frank E. Young (Grand Rapids: William B. Eerdsmans Publishing Co., 1997), p. 25.
6. Maranto, *Quest for Perfection*, pp. 139-40.
7. The United States Holocaust Memorial Museum, *Victims of the Nazis: 1933-1945*, n.p.
8. *Victims of the Nazis: 1933-1945*, n.p.
9. Task Force for U. S. Preventive Services, *Guide to Clinical Preventive Services*, 2d ed., volume 10, no. 4, 1996. The financial estimate is based on 1998 figures.
10. Hessel Bouma III, "Glossary of Genetic Terms," in Genetic Ethics, p. 268.
11. Bouma, "The Search for Shalom," in *Genetic Ethics*, pp. 14-16.
12. "Euthanasia," *Microsoft Encarta 1994*. Microsoft (register trademark) Encarta. Copyright (copyright mark) 1993 Microsoft Corporation. Copyright (copyright mark) 1993 Funk & Wagnall's Corporation.
13. *Victims of the Nazis: 1933-1945*, n.p.
14. *Victims of the Nazis: 1933-1945*, n.p.
15. Laurence Rees, *The Nazis: A Warning from History* (New York: The New Press, 1997), p. 81.
16. *Victims of the Nazis: 1933-1945*, n.p.
17. *Victims of the Nazis: 1933-1945*, n.p.

Chapter Eleven

1. *Merriam-Webster's Collegiate Dictionary*, 10th ed., see "compassion."

2. This verse became kind of a formula for describing the Lord's character throughout the Old Testament (see Num. 14:18; Neh. 9:17, 31; Ps. 86:15, 103:8, 145:8; Joel 2:13; Jonah 4:2).
3. Stanley Hauerwas, Suffering Presence: *Theological Reflections on Medicine, the Mentally Handicapped, and the Church* (Notre Dame, Ind.: University of Notre Dame Press, 1986), p. 167.
4. Donald P. McNeill, Douglas A. Morrison, and Henri J. M. Nouwen, *Compassion: A Reflection on the Christian Life* (New York: Doubleday, Image Books, 1982), pp. 20-21.
5. Pastoral Statement of U. S. Catholic Bishops on People with Disabilities, November 16, 1978, points 12 and 13.
6. Eugene H. Peterson, *The Message: The New Testament in Contemporary English* (Colorado Springs: NavPress, 1993), pp. 480-481.

Chapter Twelve

1. Joni Eareckson Tada, *Heaven: Your Real Home* (Grand Rapids: Zondervan Publishing House, 1995), p. 112.
2. Gerald Sittser, *A Grace Disguised: How the Soul Grows through Loss* (Grand Rapids: Zondervan Publishing House, 1996), p. 78.
3. Tada, *Heaven*, p. 103.
4. Eugene H. Peterson, The Message: *The New Testament in Contemporary English* (Colorado Springs: NavPress, 1993), pp. 366, 367.

Resource List

Books

Christian Parenting

Extraordinary Kids: nurturing and championing your child with special needs
By Cheri Fuller and Louise Tucker Jones, copyright 1997
Focus on the Family Publishing, Colorado Springs, CO 80995
Practical advice on how o best advocate for your child with special needs.
Includes chapters on finding a network of support, prayer, siblings and placement issues..

I'll Love You Forever: Accepting Your Child When Your Expectations are Unfulfilled
By Norm and Joyce Wright, copyright 1993 Focus on the Family Publishing, Colorado Springs, CO 80995
Deals with the emotional aspect of parenting a child with special needs and circumstances based on personal experience of being both a Christian counselor and a parent of a child with special needs.

Our Special Child: A Parent's Guide to Helping Children with Special Needs Reach Their Potential by Bette M. Ross, M.Ed., copyright 1993 by Oliver-Nelson Books, a division of Thomas Nelson, Inc., Nashville, Tennessee
Based on personal stories of parenting a child with Down Syndrome, the author guides parents step-by-step through each of the challenges a child with special needs faces.

<u>Living with a Challenging Child: Hope for Mother of Children with ADD, Hyperactivity, or Other Behavioral Problems </u>by Jayne Ray Garrison, copyright 1996, Vine Books, an imprint of Servant Publications, P.O. Box 8617, Ann Arbor, Michigan 48107
Each chapter begins with a "confession" about the frustrations of raising a child with behavioral problems, and follows with scriptural encouragements and ends with a section on "practical advice" for coping.

Eternal Perspective

<u>When God Weeps: Why Our Sufferings Matter to the Almighty </u>by Joni Eareckson Tada Tada and Steven Estes, copyright 1997, ZondervanPublishingHouse, Grand Rapids, Michigan 49530
Addresses the difficult questions associated with suffering and faith. Asks the "forbidden" questions and answers with solid biblical teaching.

<u>Heaven: Your Real Home </u>by Joni Eareckson Tada, copyright 1995, ZondervanPublishingHouse, Grand Rapids, Michigan 49530
Using scripture, paints a realistic picture of a realm that often seems unreal to us.

<u>A Grace Disguised: How the Soul Grows Through Loss</u> by Gerald L. Sittser, copyright 1996, ZondervanPublishingHouse, Grand Rapids, Michigan 49530
Using the author's experience of losing close family members, including his wife and several children in an auto accident, takes the reader through grief to a better understanding of God's character.

General Parenting

From the Heart: On Being the Mother of a Child with Special Needs Edited by Jayne D.B. Marsh copyright 1994 by the University of Southern Maine. First Woodbine House edition 1995, Woodbine House, 6510 Bells Mill Road, Bethesda, Maryland 20817
Interviews with mothers who parent children with a variety of disabilities reveal the heartaches and triumphs of living with disability.

Parent Survival Manual: A Guide to Crisis Resolution in Autism and Related Developmental Disorders edited by Eric Schopler, copyright 1995 Plenum Press, 233 Spring Street, New York, NY 10013
Offers sound, practical advice in handling the most stubborn behavioral difficulties often associated with autism and related disorders.

The Early Intervention Dictionary: A Multidisciplinary Guide to Terminology by Jeanine G. Coleman, M.Ed., copyright 1993 Woodbine House, 6510 Bells Mill Road, Bethesda, Maryland 20817
Dictionary filled with explanation of terms and anacronyms (sp? Right word?) related to disability, special education and medical procedures and equipment. Invaluable to the parent of a newly diagnosed child.

Changed by a Child: Companion Notes for Parents of a Child with a Disability
Short reflections on the aspects of raising a child with special needs. Excellent use of quotes by parents and authors. Contains poetic writing with an occasional "raw" word that may offend some readers.

Specific Disability

<u>Autism: The Facts </u>by Dr. Simon Baron-Cohen and Dr. Patrick Bolton copyright 1993 Oxford University Press, Walton Street, Oxford OX2 6DP

<u>Dyslexia & Other Learning Difficulties: The Facts </u>by Mark Selikowitz copyright 1993 Oxford University Press, Walton Street, Oxford OX2 6DP

<u>Tourette Syndrome: The Facts</u> by Mary Robertson and Simon Baron-Cohen copyright 1998 Oxford University Press, Great Clarendon Street, Oxford OX2 6DP
Other books in "<u>The Facts</u>" series include, <u>Epilepsy</u> by Anthony Hopkins and Richard Appleton, <u>Head Injury</u> by Dorothy Gronwall, Philip Wrightson and Peter Waddell, <u>Muscular Dystrophy</u> by Alan E.H. Emery, <u>Obsessive-Compulsive Disorder</u> by Padmal de Silva and Stanley Rachman, <u>Down Syndrome</u> by Mark Selikowitz

<u>Children with Autism: A Parents' Guide</u> Edited by Michael D. Powers, Psy.D. copyright 1989 by Woodbine House, 5615 Fishers Lane, Rockville, MD 20852

<u>Children with Tourette Sydrome: A Parents' Guide</u> Edited by Tracy Haerle copyright 1992 by Woodbine House, 5615 Fishers Lane, Rockville, MD 20852
There are other Parent Guides on specific disability in this *The Special Needs Collection.*

<u>The World of the Autistic Child: Understanding and Treating Autistic Spectrum Disorders </u>by Bryna Siegel copyright 1996 by Oxford University Press, Inc. 198 Madison Avenue, New York, New York 10016

<u>Right-Brained Children in a Left-Brained World:</u>
<u>Unlocking the Potential of Your ADD Child</u> by Jeffrey
Freed, M.A.T., and Laurie Parsons copyright 1997 Simon
and Schuster, Rockefeller Center, 1230 Avenue of the
Americas, New York, New York 10020

Scripture Reference List

Unless otherwise marked, all Scripture quotes
are from the NIV.
Scriptures in brackets { } are referenced, not quoted.

Introduction

(none)

Chapter 1: Not What We Expected

Psalm 62:5 (KJV)
Jeremiah 29:11
Psalm 127:3—5 (NASB)
Chapter 2: The Struggle of Diagnosis
Romans 11:33b—34
Psalm 145:8—9, 13b—14
Jeremiah 31:3
Romans 5:8
Psalm 136:1b

Chapter 3: Whose Fault Is This? Looking for Someone to Blame

John 9:2—3
Mark 11:25—26
Romans 5:10
Ephesians 2:5
Matthew 5:45
Luke 13:1—5
John 9:1—3
Job 1:7, 11—12
{Psalm 51:5}
Exodus 4:11
Deuteronomy 32:39
Isaiah 45:6b—7
Isaiah 14:24
Lamentations 3:32—33
Psalm 66:12b

Chapter 4: The Crucible of Shock, Denial, and Grief

Psalm 34:18
{Genesis 3:8—10}

Psalm 30:5
Job 2:10
{Ephesians 4:32}
{Psalm 147:3}
{2 Corinthians 1:3—4}
Isaiah 53:3—5
Hebrews 12:2—3
Hebrews 4:15a, 16

Chapter 5: Fear and Faith

Psalm 40:2
Matthew 10:28, {29—31}
John 14:27
Matthew 6:9—10
Isaiah 40:27—28
Psalm 103:14
{Ephesians 6:16}
Isaiah 41:13

Chapter 6: The Dark Side: Envy and Anger

James 3:13—14; Ephesians 4:26—27
{2 Corinthians 12:20}
{Galatians 5:20}
{Ephesians 4:26—27}
John 21:18—19, 22
Psalm 90:11
Job 37:20—22 (The Message)
{Matthew 10:30}
Psalm 51:6 (NASB)
Ephesians 4:26—27 (The Message)
Genesis 32:24—30
Psalm 103:8
John 6:29
John 14:2
{1 Corinthians 3:10—15}
{1 Peter 1:7}
Revelation 7:17
{Revelation 21:1—5}

Chapter 7: Perfected in Weakness

2 Corinthians 12:9
2 Corinthians 12:6—10 (Message)
Isaiah 40:28—29
Matthew 5:3—5

Chapter 8: The Language Barrier

 1 Corinthians 14:10
 {Isaiah 55:8—9}
 Romans 8:25—28
 Revelation 19:6—7a (NRSV)

Chapter 9: Alienation and Judgment: Challenges in Our Quest to Belong

 Psalm 69:8
 Matthew 7:1—2, 5 (Message)
 {Ephesians 4:29}
 {Ephesians 2:4—8}
 {Exodus 22:21}
 {Exodus 23:12}
 {Leviticus 19:10, 34}
 {Numbers 15:16}
 {Deuteronomy 26:12}
 Ephesians 2:13
 John 1:10—11
 Isaiah 53:3
 Philippians 3:20
 1 Peter 2:11
 Colossians 3:3
 Romans 3:26
 Galatians 6:4—5, 7—9 (Message)

Chapter 10: We Have Work to Do (Part 1)

 Ephesians 5:15—16
 Revelation 3:14b, 17
 Matthew 5:3
 Matthew 18:3
 2 Corinthians 5:17—18
 Revelation 3:18—20

Chapter 11: We Have Work to Do (Part 2)

 Ephesians 2:10
 Luke 14:12—14
 {Luke 14:16—21}
 Genesis 1:27
 Psalm 139:13, 15—16
 Jeremiah 1:5
 {Genesis 1:3, 10, 12, 18, 21, 25}
 Genesis 1:31
 Leviticus 19:14
 {Deuteronomy 27:18}
 Psalm 89:14
 {Deuteronomy 32:4}
 Proverbs 14:31
 Proverbs 21:3
 Proverbs 31:8—9
 Jeremiah 22:16

Exodus 4:11
Psalm 139:14
Exodus 34:6
Deuteronomy 4:31a (NASB)
Psalm 72:13 (NASB)
Psalm 103:2a, 4
Psalm 116:5—6
Isaiah 30:181
Matthew 9:12—13 (NASB)
Matthew 9:36
Mark 1:41—42
1 Corinthians 1:26—31
{Jeremiah 9:23—24}
Zechariah 4:6

{Deuteronomy 24:17}
Ezekiel 34:15—16a
Zechariah 7:8—10
{Isaiah 1:17}
{Micah 6:8}
Luke 11:42a
Acts 20:35
 Thessalonians 5:14
Galatians 6:9
{Proverbs 22:6}
Luke 6:36 (NEB)
Colossians 3:12
James 2:5—6a, 12—13 (Message)

Chapter 12: Putting It into Perspective

Romans 5:3—5a
2 Corinthians 1:3—4
1 Corinthians 15:19 (LB)
Isaiah 35:4—6
Isaiah 35:10
1 Corinthians 13:12
1 Corinthians 15:58; 16:13—14 (Message)
2 Corinthians 4:16—18 (LB)

Scriptures in Biblical Order

Old Testament

{Genesis 1:3, 10, 12, 18, 21, 25} (ch. 11)
Genesis 1:31 (ch. 11)
Genesis 1:27 (ch. 11)
{Genesis 3:8—10} (ch. 4)
Genesis 32:24—30 (ch. 6)

Exodus 4:11 (ch. 3)
*Exodus 4:11 (ch. 11)
{Exodus 22:21} (ch. 9}
{Exodus 23:12} (ch. 9)
Exodus 34:6 (ch. 11)

{Leviticus 19:10, 34} (ch. 9)
Leviticus 19:14 (ch. 11)
{Isaiah 1:17} (ch. 11)
{Numbers 15:15} (ch. 9)
Isaiah 30:18 (ch. 11)

Psalm 103:14 (ch. 5)
Psalm 116:5—6 (ch. 11)
Psalm 127:3—5 (ch. 1)
Psalm 136:1b (ch. 2)
Psalm 139:13, 15—16 (ch. 11)
Psalm 139:14 (ch. 11)
Psalm 145:8—9, 13b—14 (ch. 2)
{Psalm 147:3} (ch. 4)

Proverbs 14:31 (ch. 11)
Proverbs 21:3 (ch. 11)
{Proverbs 22:6} (ch. 11)
Proverbs 31:8—9 (ch. 11)

Isaiah 14:24 (ch. 3)

Scripture Reference List

Deuteronomy 4:31a (ch. 11)
{Deuteronomy 24:17} (ch. 11)
{Deuteronomy 26:12} (ch. 9)
{Deuteronomy 27:18} (ch. 11)
{Deuteronomy 32:4} (ch. 11)
Deuteronomy 32:39 (ch. 3)

Job 1:7, 11—12 (ch. 3)
Job 2:10 (ch. 4)
Job 37:20—22 (ch. 6)

Psalm 30:5 (ch. 4)
Psalm 34:18 (ch. 4)
Psalm 40:2 (ch. 5)
{Psalm 51:5} (ch. 3)
Psalm 51:6 (ch. 6)
Psalm 62:5 (ch. 1)
Psalm 66:12b (ch. 3)
Psalm 69:8 (ch. 9)
Psalm 72:13 (ch. 11)
Psalm 89:14 (ch. 11)
Psalm 90:11 (ch. 6)
Psalm 103:2a, 4 (ch. 11)
Psalm 103:8 (ch. 6)

Isaiah 35:4—6 (ch. 12)
Isaiah 35:10 (ch. 12)
Isaiah 40:27—28 (ch. 5)
Isaiah 40:28—29 (ch. 7)
Isaiah 41:13 (ch. 5)
Isaiah 45:6b—7 (ch. 3)
Isaiah 53:3 (ch. 9)
Isaiah 53:3—5 (ch. 4)
{Isaiah 55:8—9} (ch. 8)

Jeremiah 1:5 (ch. 11)
{Jeremiah 9:23—24} (ch. 11)
Jeremiah 22:16 (ch. 11)
Jeremiah 29:11 (ch. 1)
Jeremiah 31:3 (ch. 2)

Lamentations 3:32—33 (ch. 3)

Ezekiel 34:15—16a (ch. 11)

{Micah 6:8} (ch. 11)

Zechariah 4:6 (ch. 11)
Zechariah 7:8—10 (ch. 11)

New Testament

Matthew 5:3 (ch. 10)2 Corinthians 1:3—4 (ch. 12 {4})
Matthew 5:3—5 (ch. 7)2 Corinthians 4:16—18 (ch. 12)
Matthew 5:45 (ch. 3)2 Corinthians 5:17—18 (ch. 10)
Matthew 6:9—10 (ch. 5)2 Corinthians 12:6—10 (ch. 7)
Matthew 7:1—2, 5 (ch. 9)2 Corinthians 12:9 (ch. 7)
Matthew 9:12—13 (ch. 11){2 Corinthians 12:20} (ch. 6)
Matthew 9:36 (ch. 11)
Matthew 10: 28, {29—31} (ch. 5){Galatians 5:20} (ch. 6)
{Matthew 10:30} (ch. 6)Galatians 6:4—5, 7—9 (ch. 9)
Matthew 18:3 (ch. 10)Galatians 6:9 (ch. 11)
Mark 1:41—42 (ch. 11){Ephesians 2:4—8} (ch. 9)
Mark 11:25—26 (ch. 3)Ephesians 2:5(ch. 3)
Ephesians 2:10 (ch. 11)
Luke 6:36 (ch. 11)Ephesians 2:13 (ch. 9)
Luke 11:42a (ch. 11)Ephesians 4:26—27 (ch. 6 - twice)
Luke 13:1—5 (ch. 3){Ephesians 4:29} (ch. 9)
Luke 14:12—14 (ch. 11){Ephesians 4:32} (ch. 4)
{Luke 14:16—21} (ch. 11)Ephesians 5:15—16 (ch. 10)
{Ephesians 6:16} (ch. 5)
John 1:10—11 (ch. 9)
John 6:29 (ch. 6)Philippians 3:20 (ch. 9)
John 9:1—3 (ch. 3)

John 9:2—3 (ch. 3)Colossians 3:3 (ch. 9)
John 14:2 (ch. 6)Colossians 3:12 (ch. 11)
John 14:27 (ch. 5)
John 21:18—19, 22 (ch. 6)1 Thessalonians 5:14 (ch. 11)
Acts 20:35 (ch. 11)Hebrews 4:15a, 16 (ch. 4)
Hebrews 12:2—3 (ch. 4)
Romans 5:3—5a (ch. 12)
Romans 3:26 (ch. 9)James 2:5—6a, 12—13 (ch. 11)
Romans 5:8 (ch. 2)James 3:13—14 (ch. 6)
Romans 5:10 (ch. 3)
Romans 8:25—28 (ch. 8){1 Peter 1:7} (ch. 6)
Romans 11:33b—34 (ch. 2)1 Peter 2:11 (ch. 9)
1 Corinthians 1:26—31 (ch. 11)Revelation 3:14b, 17 (ch. 10)
{1 Corinthians 3:10—15} (ch. 6)Revelation 3:18—20 (ch. 10)
1 Corinthians 13:12 (ch. 12)Revelation 7:17 (ch. 6)
1 Corinthians 14:10 (ch. 8)Revelation 19:6—7a (ch. 8)
1 Corinthians 15:19 (ch. 12){Revelation 21:1—5} (ch. 6)
1 Corinthians 15:58; 16:13—14 (ch. 12)